The Status Game II
Dashboards and Gages

MARK BRADFORD

Copyright © 2018 Mark Bradford

The Status Game™ and Spark Point™ are trademarks of Mark Bradford.

Printed in the United States of America
First Printing, 2018

Remarkable Books
Alchemy

ISBN: 1948326035
ISBN-13: 978-1948326032
Library of Congress: 2018949976

www.thestatusgame.com

v1.1

MARK BRADFORD

DEDICATION

To those that scream "This makes no sense" or "Why is she with him" or "Why do you like douchebags?!" or "Oh my god I need a drink."

To those who thirst for knowledge and seek first to understand. Everyone who hurts, everyone who experiences frustration - this is for you.

To you, the person who asks questions others do not. To you, the person who simply wants to connect with another human being, do the right thing and live happily every after. I dedicate this to you, because you are who I wrote this book for.

CONTENTS

MARK BRADFORD

ACKNOWLEDGMENTS

Coffee for the consistency it gives my life, and the buzz I still get from it especially when I am up at an ungodly hour writing in a cafe that has the music way too loud.

Tea for the comfort it gives me while it makes me believe I'm drinking something extra healthy like I'm some sort of monk who only puts the goodness of mother nature in his body instead of the energy bars that are 61% old newspapers.

Martinis because they are elegant and teach us that it is about the slow, smoldering journey as you chat with friends or really attractive women.

To low hops beer because it's everything martinis are not, and that's OK too.

My kids for the love they fill me with while they drive me crazy. Rosie and Jacqui for their unfaltering support, Jeff for the slice of wisdom we share each Friday, Scott for his kindred spirit, and Mark for his motivating words - telling me that my chance of making money at this is equal to his chance of winning the lottery.

I'd like to thank understanding people who make an effort to understand a concept before their lizard brain yells "Oh no! No no no!" and closes the Big Doors of Understanding.

If it wasn't for *The Status Game* - which allowed me to reveal this concept and lay the groundwork - without which I could never expand upon and write The Status Game II.

Yeah, I acknowledged a bunch of beverages, then people, then a book.

WELCOME BACK

Welcome back to anyone who is here because of *The Status Game* (the first book). That book laid some groundwork, but mostly provided entertaining tips and information regarding on line dating. This book, however, is pure status. It is also self-inclusive - and will explain status from the ground up - what it is, how it works, how it controls you and your relationships, and what you can do with it.

You'll find some very tangible information about such things as status, validation, vulnerability and even douchebaggery. As always, I present this to you like a text book would so that you can reference it. It's factual stuff. It's useable information.

It is not, however, a 'what to do when this happens' sort of book.

It's not advice, it's the mechanics of reality.

Why it is a game will help you to understand how our brains play tricks, and how you can be an active player instead of being played.

Ha Ha I'm Married will show how your' status continues to be important, and just may give you the info necessary to save your marriage.

Lather, Rinse, Repeat will help you to deal with, understand and move through a break up in a way that is less painful and better for your sanity.

Validation will show you how incredibly powerful that feeling can be, and very well may explain some bizarre actions on your part or your loved ones.

Confidence, Arrogance, Douchebaggery and Status will open your eyes to why you keep picking someone who is, well, sort of a dick.

The *Link Juice* chapter will even give you suggestions on how you can use what you learn here to get more stuff out of life - fun stuff.

MORE ON STATUS

You know, I just love how that sounds, right? Read that title out loud. *More On Status*. I love the phonetics of that - but then I love that sort of thing anyway.

I believe that a bit more needs to be said on what 'status' actually is. As I mentioned, the previous book laid some groundwork, but I'm going to lay that groundwork again for you. In addition, in speaking with other people about 'status' I found that there was a lot of confusion.

What is status again?

Status is not *stature*. It is not your stature in the community. It is not what a mover and shaker you are, how much money you have, how big your house is or how much power you wield in your particular organization. To that last point I found it very interesting that those that were very involved in their church immediately - upon hearing me talk about 'status' - would jump in and say they knew exactly what I was talking about. They didn't. Instead they thought I meant all the above - the big house, the prominent figure, the power. They were very concerned and aware of those people in their church for

5

some reason.

Status is a separate neutral thing that *includes* all that stuff for some people. But status is simply a gage, a gage for whatever thing(s) is(are) important to you.

If you are driving your car you see a set of status gages for all the important stuff - how much fuel you have, the oil pressure (if your car's not electric), the temperature, the miles you've put on it. All those things are important, which is why those gages are right in your face.

So, instead of saying "how much gas the car has is important to me" you just say "I want to make sure I have enough gas" and "I'm running on fumes and I don't like that." or "A full tank makes me feel safe and secure." Gasoline is a status item - both in how much you currently have and your capacity.

In that same way, weight, attractiveness, security, height, healthiness, age, etc. are all status items and gages on your virtual dashboard. So...

Status item = a Gage.

Get it now?

You're used to people using the word 'status' to mean 'gage' but the way it's used is misleading and hidden. 'Martial status' refers to a gage that measures *married, single, divorced, separated*, etc. 'Community status' is a gage to measure how someone is regarded in their community and the needle can point to *unknown, harmless, well known, upstanding, pillar, weirdo*, etc.

No one says 'height status' or 'attractiveness status' but instead they just say *tall, short, hot, cute, not very* etc.

It means the same thing. I'm just making you aware of what gages you put on your dashboard of life.

Perhaps I should have called this chapter 'Status: Dashboard of Life' so you wouldn't be smiling at 'Moron Status.' Regardless, hopefully you get it now.

So let's revisit your status items - the gages on your dashboard. What are they?

Is height important to you? Are you a woman looking for a really tall guy?

Is weight important to you? Are you a guy that needs to have a girl that is super fit?

Is money important to you? Are you a woman that finds a man with a lot of money very attractive and like the owner of the car with a full tank of gas you feel secure, safe and happy?

I just picked a few of the most common status items for people. There are many more. Some are based on nature; others on nurture. Some are enforced by drama; others by confirmation bias.

If there are a bunch of gages on my dashboard, and gages on his dashboard, we just choose based on who makes the needles go the highest right?

There's more to it than that.

So when you are choosing someone, you choose based on where those needles are. In our car example, each gage is important but some are more important than others.

Imagine this:
There are a number of cars sitting there. Each one is cool

looking, some are more cool looking than others. You pick the really sporty looking one because one of your gages is 'attractive to others.' This means it's a big deal to you to have your car/girlfriend/boyfriend turn heads. It makes you feel special and elevates how you feel about yourself. Someone with a cool car must have a lot of money and be really cool. Someone with a hot boyfriend must be pretty special to have a guy like that want to be seen with her.

So you pick the hot, sporty model.

When you get in the car, you notice the gas is almost empty. That concerns you. Though it's a cool car, having very little gas makes you feel unsafe. On top of that the gas tank is tiny; even if you filled it to the top you'd only get a few miles out of it.

This is unacceptable to you. You find that it's more important that you can count on this car and be safe and not be worrying that you're going to run out of gas all the time, than having it turn heads. It's not worth it. Maybe you'd drive it for one night…

Real life equivalent: A hot person who has a crappy job and doesn't seem to have much ambition.

Your friend comes over to pick a car. She is 'out there' in your opinion and you can't figure out her type. She looks at all the cars equally, and their appearance doesn't seem to matter. She gets into one, and frowns and gets out. Then she gets in one that you think is really plain and boring, and after looking at the dashboard, she gets out and walks around it, paying particular attention to the big, knobby tires. She jumps back in and says she loves it.

She picked this car - you learn later - because it has a special shifter, can drive on the highway and do off road stuff. The gas tank is huge ands gets surprisingly good MPG. She feels safe, and the car is versatile, and relatively cheap to operate.

Real life equivalent: She likes guys that have a lot of stamina, are practical, have a really good head on their shoulders, are good earners and like going away for camping weekends without showering. Someone that doesn't care that she doesn't wear makeup most of the time. Their appearance plays very little part in choice.

So you go to another car that's sporty enough on the outside. The seats are cramped. You get into this car. It's got a full big tank, and you notice the speedometer goes to 200. Holy crap. So you take it out for a test drive and the car struggles to get past 90. You return, frustrated. It looks like a sporty car, but it's not.

Real life equivalent: Arrogant instead of confident. Big tall guy, giant white teeth. All talk.

I could go on and on with these car metaphors. But you get it, right? Does she ever find the right car? You'll see at the end of the book.

Understanding the gages on your dashboard helps you to figure out why you are attracted to the people you are attracted to. Or - equally as important - why you just get no spark with someone you think you should. That can be and is frustrating and you end up beating yourself up.

The examples demonstrate that the initial attractiveness is what makes you want to get into the car. Then once in, you take it for a test drive, and you see the gages. Like real life you don't get to know the inside until later - which is why you might date someone only to find that they are a terrible match.

Then you beat yourself up.

Don't beat yourself up[1].

---

[1] Rule #1. See glossary.

Mark Bradford

WHY IT IS A GAME

OK, so we clarified the 'Status' part of *'The Status Game'* so let's clarify why it's a 'game.'

As I said we use these gages. So we just pick someone who has the right setting on the right gages, right? Well, life isn't that simple. Like the sporty car that said it went to 200, sometimes the gages lie. And sometimes you do too - to yourself, and others. And they do the same.

Everyone is playing the game, subconsciously (as a protective measure) or consciously because their awareness allows them to.

This is not to say that everyone is a big stinkin' lying cheater. But, if you could cheat and win the lottery would you? If you could be given, say, three of the numbers each time to give you an advantage would you take that? Or if you found that the lottery required you to write six numbers into the boxes but up till now you were writing only three wouldn't you appreciate that knowledge?

It's a game because we can make a conscious effort to be

aware of it. It's a game because it's a sort of challenge and has a winner/loser sometimes. It's a game because there is a certain surreal aspect of it, like being in a club with dumb rules. You say to yourself and others "Let's just be good to each other, let's be nice people and everything will work out." Unfortunately the presence of your awareness will not automatically cause theirs to be just as present. Your perception may be different than theirs. The amount of influence the status items have may be more than you or they can handle. It just may be too much and then the game is lost by you and won by the new person. Or you may want to stay with your boyfriend but you just can't get over the weight gain, job loss, or lack of interest in stuff you now find important.

So it's a game when you realize that all the perception, awareness, self control and higher level thinking are no match for simple, deep visceral status items that control your feelings.

He who controls the spark controls the relationship. And the 'he' in question is your status items.

When you realize that as long as you stay fit you stay together, or that the thing that really means something to you - for some bizarre reason - is a very simple thing, it makes you question just how evolved of a human you are. It makes you question your own brain. It makes you question love.

Don't do that. Don't let the game play you. Just remember that status items drive you, and that you are the one looking at the gages.

If you really feel like you are being lead down the wrong path again and again by your items, don't ignore them.

Ignoring them makes things worse and they will just exert

more control over you with a vengeance. No, instead of trying to control them, *explore* them. Dig deeper. Figure out the *why*, and you will gain more control. So instead of questioning THAT you like tall guys, figure out WHY you like tall guys. Maybe you really value security and tall = security. And then you find yourself dating a tall guy with a crappy job with no ambition and say "what did I ever see in him?"

So what then? Well you can either just pursue security and ignore the height thing, or just make sure that the tall guys that turn your crank all have decent jobs and can fill the security role for you.

Or it's just a physical thing - a lining up of heads and chests and naughty bits. And that's that.

Or you're a guy who goes for younger chicks. Is it that you enjoy being with someone who has no clue about the TV shows you grew up with, or is it because you like women with more energy and women who are ten years younger are a better fun energy match for you? Regardless, that information is priceless, and can help you feel better about being you.

Feel better about being you. Doesn't that sound like the opposite of beating yourself up?

Good. Let's do that from now on.

STATUS HAS A SECOND MEANING

Oh jeez. We just clarified all this and now you have to learn that status has two meanings? Forget it. No no, it's easy. It relates to status, and the game at the same time and I can sum it up in two words before you run away:

"Status Quo"

the existing state of affairs, especially regarding social or political issues.

You've heard this. You know what it means for the most part, right? Let me define it again and risk insulting your intelligence.

It means **the way things are right now**. If you are in a relationship, the status quo is how things are, how things work, and how you believe things to be.

As long as the status quo is maintained your relationship works and you are happy.

The same can be said for your mate. He is also happy as

long as the status quo is maintained.

Based on that description all relationships should last forever right? Unfortunately that isn't true, because there are a number of things that complicate this.

Complication #1: The status quo for him is not the same as Status Quo for her (your gages are different than his).

Each person has their own status items. When you get in his car, you want to see certain gages. When he gets into your car, the gages he wants to see may be different. They may be the same, but more likely they are different and may be completely different. This is why you may see a really attractive person with an unattractive person, in your humble opinion of course - not mine, that would be rude.

It's because one person values something you can't see, etc. This is also touched on in "Interdimensional Math" in *The Status Game*. and revisited here in "Interdimensional Math Revisited." Well, what did you expect it to be called?

In each relationship we have two status quo's with some possible overlap, kind of like a Venn Diagram.

You may have two people with exactly the same status items, or at least they have a giant gage for the same thing. For example two people who value a religious belief above all else - as long as they both strongly, unfalteringly believe this thing they are madly in love with each other. The other stuff just doesn't matter, or is vastly less important. Yes, this is not only very possible but happens all the time - a relationship is based on a common devotion to a thing or cause. Think of anti-war hippies from the 60s, dude. Or a couple you know that are very prominent members of their church. What else do you like? Oh, nothing? They only talk about being a prominent member of their church? Or two people who like to ride. Or two people who like to SCUBA for some reason. This happens in all sorts of relationships. You have at least one friend that says "I was with Bob because we were both so into [insert thing] but boy he was a dick.

More likely you both have some overlapping items, and one person adds up their gages, and the other adds up their respective and different gages.

Because we have two different status quo's we have two different requirements for behaviors and maintenance.

If her main status items are height and financial security, as long as it looks like he is maintaining this wealth - and not making dumb financial decisions - she's cool. His status quo is maintained with her, and he ain't gettin' any shorter so that's an easy one for him.

For him, as long as she stays attractive, and showers him with a lot of affection, her status quo is maintained with him. Yes, there's a spark involved - remember we are already past that part - we are talking about status quo now.

So, two separate *requirements*. Two separate (to some extent) things that have to be *maintained*.

Complication #2: Status quo changes over time (what the gages say).

When you are in a certain part of your life, your wants, needs, desires and beliefs reflect that. Most people evolve. Things happen. You go from being a wide eyed college kid, to someone who has to pay bills, to someone who has kids and would push anyone down a flight of stairs that would harm them, to someone who is finally an empty nester and Jesus I'm so glad those kids are gone I just want to have fun now and spend my own money on me.

You can imagine that these life changes affect the status quo in a relationship.

If Attractive To Others or Attractiveness, or Fitness is really important to you, then your mate getting older may be affected and his/her gage goes down.

If you're realistic about these items, then you get that a 50 year old person may look different than a 25 year old, and can be just as hot and sexy and - on some dimensions - even more so[2].

If not, then you start sniffin' around for a younger person - because the status quo isn't being *maintained*.

Or, if your mate lets themselves go - perhaps they gained 30 lbs because they became sedentary, which is due to the fact that they are bored, which is because you take such good care of them.

Or she had three kids and jumping on a treadmill ain't #1 on her list, since all you do is work and she's essentially a full time mom and you want what now?

Regardless of the circumstances, if the gages go down, or if your interest in a particular gage changes, the statuses also change.

Complication #3: The status gages desired change over time (what gages appear in the car).

As you move to different phases in your life, understandably and predictably your status items change as well. Things that weren't important when you were wild and single and care free at 23 are now immensely important to you. Just as likely there are things you were

---

[2] Oh hi...you come here often? I'm Mark.

passionate about that have lost their meaning - through experiences.

Experiences equals mistakes, mistakes equals wisdom and wisdom changes your gages.

If he really values attractiveness, but now that he's older and wiser really values intelligence and independence, all of a sudden his extremely hot wife just doesn't have the status items she needs. He doesn't give her the memo that the gages have changed and he files for divorce.

Though her Hotness gage is still high, the newly introduced Independence and Intelligence gages are not.

He hadn't picked her on those items, but now he is assessing her on them. Fair? Nope.

However, if he had chosen her on a combination of Hotness, Intelligence and Independence, then the perceived reduction in Hotness plays far less of a part, especially if he evolves to appreciate the latter two gages.

Equally as likely is that though she had always been an independent smarty pants, he never noticed that when he wanted to be with all that hotness. Lucky for him when he became more mature and those gages became bigger, the needles are pretty high on them.

Things like this happen all the time in relationships over time - gages shrink, grow, disappear and appear.

Sometimes people say they grow apart - which is due to new gages appearing that were never there before, and the other person barely registers on those newly important gages.

Sometimes people cheat, because their new gages that

appear drive them so strongly away that they don't muster the self control to have an honest discussion. That's not the only reason people cheat - mostly it's because they are big giant poopy heads.

Realizing that there are these complications helps you to appreciate how relationships work and how there is a constant motion in your wants, needs, desires and requirements. Those gages control your destiny as much as you will let them. Sometimes more.

It's a balance between giving yourself exactly what the gages want, remaining faithful to promises that included lots of drinking and partying and possible embarrassing stories said into a microphone, and understanding that life is give and take.

Finding someone who is right for you

I don't know about you but I never liked this phrase. It always sounds like it's being said by a know-it-all person who wants you to settle for someone that you don't think is fantastic. "She's not right for you" sounds like "She's way too attractive for someone like you." Finding someone 'right' never sounds like an exciting thing to pursue. If you walked into a club and saw a whole bunch of attractive people and surveyed that crowd, you would feel weird if you said "someone out there is right for me."

Weird. Boring.

Instead you want to find someone who is awesome, sexy, amazing, interesting, exciting. All those words that make for a great movie make for that person you want to find.

If your status gages are Height, Kindness, Intelligence, Leadership and Dad Material, you look into that crowd hoping to find that hot tall guy who will have really smart conversation with you. You're eyes go wide at the prospect of looking up at this cute guy who makes your head swim with his smartness, which you sorely need. You think about dancing slowly at the end of the night as you joke about kids and you love his answers - so warm, so kind. The thought of him revealing that he does quite well at his job and seems to always slip into leadership roles makes your knees weak - *a guy that I can hand over some control to, finally*.

That all sounds pretty exciting, doesn't it? But that paragraph just described you finding someone who is 'right for you.'

Finding someone who is 'right' for you gets a terrible rap. And like 'status' it has a whole different, deeper meaning.

They are right for you because they are high on all your status gages. You are right for them because you are high on all their status gages. You two are perfect for each other.

Your instincts guide you to those people who are high on your gages, but you may not know why. You may not be consciously aware of these gages.

If you know people who have absolute train wreck relationships they are undoubtedly either completely unaware of their gages or in denial about them. Not only do they not delve deeper into the *why* of a gage, they are clueless as to what's actually *on* their dashboard. They don't think past the initial seven second attraction spark.

It's a great way to have train wreck relationships for the rest of your life - this denial and lack of awareness. It behooves you not to do this. The more effort you put into figuring out your gages, the easier it will be to find that person who is right for you. See? You just had that same distaste in reading "right for you." It's OK, I felt it as I wrote it.   You know what I mean now. That person that excites you, turns your crank, gives you butterflies, the person that makes you feel really lucky to have - all that.

The important bullet points to take away from this is as follows:

- Understand that we all have status gages. Everyone.
- Your status gages are probably not exactly the same as hers/his and that's OK.
- Your gages will grow and shrink over time and that's OK.
- Some gages may appear and some may go away over time and thats OK.
- Some of your gages are actually indicators of the real gage (as in the tall = security common issue).
- There are complications to these gages.
- Your gages exert a tremendous amount of control over you.
- If you do not give the gages proper respect and understanding you will find your actions to be not of your own volition - meaning you're gonna do stuff, or question your sanity/faithfulness/maturity. It means that self control is going to be a real problem.
- A lack of awareness of gages leads to horrible train wreck relationships and repeating the same pains over and over again.
- The more you know about your gages, the easier it will be to find someone who is truly 'right' for you
- Delving into the why of a gage helps you to discover the true gage behind it sometimes.

Mark Bradford

WHAT ARE MY GAGES?

I touched in the importance of knowing what your status items were in *The Status Game*. Now that we have defined them with more clarity - i.e. - status gages on your virtual dashboard - you want to know exactly how to figure these out.

If you could snap your fingers and have your virtual dashboard appear wouldn't you? Snap, poof, there it is. Some big gages, some smaller ones - all laid out for you. There is nothing misleading, it's all there and perfectly clear for you.

You stare at it, maybe smirk a little, "I knew that... and that." Your eyes widen a little. "OK, that one I didn't know." It's all becoming clear to you - your actions, why you pick certain people, even why you took a new job, or moved to a certain part of the city, or hang out with certain people.

Wow. These gages really do control what you do, what you seek.

Now that you see them clearly you are able to better understand yourself. Instinctively, your mind wanders to your current relationship. You think of him or her and how they affect your gages. Makes sense. Perhaps one of the gages doesn't make sense - this person registers a zero on it, yet you have warm fuzzies. Then you realize that the gage is pretty small, and they register a solid seven on the biggest of your gages.

You understand that this big gage easily trumps a bunch of the little ones.

With these gages in front of you, you can now see exactly the kind of person that would be right for you.

So how do we figure this out in the real world? Can we just visualize this dashboard an see the gages? Will you even be aware of all of your gages?

As I've said you may not be aware of everything important to you because some of it is nature, some of it is nurture, and some of it is just fucking crazy.

Sorry, it is. It really is. Things happen to us that make us swing a certain way to overcompensate.

So what can we do to determine our gages? Well there are a few things we can do to that end.

Visit your track record

It stands to reason that your dashboard lead you to your previous relationships. Therefore if we look at them we may have a clue as to what your gages say, or as to what you believe they say.

If you are the average person you have had a respectable number of relationships. By respectable I mean "more than three" and "less than 254."

If so then you have enough from which to gain some useful data.

For this part to work it is important that you turn off the part of your brain that 'knows better' and 'gets it.' This is not an active exercise - it is a forensic study in static, unchanging, dead data. What I mean is that we are going to objectively look at what you've done in the past. We are not going to try to reason or interpret what we see. That will surely mess up the results and continue to keep you in the dark, which is the opposite of why we are doing that.

So get with the program and turn off that part of you, Mr. Knowitall.

Thinking back on a previous relationship, what got you together? What was the initial spark that made you talk to her/him? And what were the circumstances of your meeting? All those can answer some questions.

If you remember from *The Status Game*, there is an initial visual spark, then we connect in one of three ways.

So, first of all, where were you when you met? This is more important than you think, because where you met them can limit or be the cause of why you like them.

For example meeting a woman in a bar is a very good lead in for gages related to status in the society and physical appearance. It can also relate heavily to intentions.

Meeting someone at work can relate to dependability, wealth, stability and relationship stamina.

If you meet someone in a bar they are probably going to be at their most attractive, as they are in their 'going out' clothing (and makeup - oooh, smokey eyes). If you have an Attractive To Others gage then this is the easiest place to go to get that data. You may get some of it at work, but you'll get a lot less at the laundromat, library or random street meeting. Meeting them at work relates to security, professionalism, intelligence, attractiveness to others.

If your gage is Sincerity, and Devotion to Spirituality you may very well have made that connection at a yoga class, a church or some sort of meeting.

This doesn't mean you can't meet these people at other locations - certainly those devout people still have to wash their clothing - it just means that your gages and your locations may line up. Habit and efficiency play a part.

And this fact may help you to determine your gages. It may also help you to determine why you may be meeting the wrong people.

So, if you aren't meeting people that show up on your gages you may be going to the wrong places. It is very possible that the kind of places and circles you move about in do not have your kind of people in it, even though it attracts you.

It may be a good idea to make some radical changes to where you go, what you do and what circles you are a part of for the purpose of meeting those individuals whose gages are important to you.

Mark Bradford

The Status Game

STATUS HAS A THIRD MEANING

Ha! I heard your brows furrow when you read that. What a neat sound - like two furry caterpillars getting jiggy, like they're sitting in a bar and one says "What are ya drinking baby?" and the other one definitely does NOT say "I have a boyfriend."

I only titled it that way to illicit that response and to test how close you're following along.

We've actually already defined the third meaning in the previous chapters - 'status quo' basically sums it up. However I wanted to distill something even further.

When I originally decided to write *The Status Game* and create the card game of the same name, there was a singular concept on my mind.

Status mean what you thought of the other person and what they thought of you. Were they worth pursuing?

Hard to get

We see the status game in action every time someone plays

hard to get. *Hard to get* means they are inflating their status so that it reinforces the impact it has on you.

If you like a girl and she knows this, she can and will increase her status even higher - like a puffer fish, or a peacock or a wizard that conjures up a couple tiny winged creatures that alight on his shoulders. In all cases it is to reinforce what you already believe.

"Yeah, that's right baby, I'm all that and even more." Puff. Unfold, Poof.

Why do this if you already have them? Why keep selling and hitting them, like the way they yell on the loudspeakers "Sunday Sunday Sunday!! Be there! At the drag way races!!" to an audience that already paid to be there.

Because status is a powerful thing. Because more status means more leverage. Because status can change and you want to give yourself that buffer. Because status is intoxicating - for both parties.

So in the case of the girl that knows the boy likes her, her next actions either stabilize her status, reduce or reinforce it. She doesn't want to reduce it.

You were probably on one end or the other in a situation like this:

Person A expresses interest in person B. Person B immediately froths over Person A. Person A's interest is almost completely destroyed.

Don't like hypothetical A & B people? Neither do I. Fucking letters. What about Doug and Cindy?

Doug is a decent looking guy, good head on his shoulders. He meets Cindy at a party. He thinks she is attractive, presentable, even kinda hot. They chat a bit and they both feel a spark.

They both think the other person's status is pretty high. This is a good thing, and how connections are made and move forward.

She expresses this attraction to him in a little light flirting. He immediately starts expressing how awesome she is. In fact he goes on and on and on about it, like he just found the meaning of life.

Cindy's face changes. The excitement drains out of her expression. It changes from hopeful excitement to minor amusement, to annoyance as if she's talking to a carpet salesman and is not in the market for new carpet. The more Doug goes on and on and talks about her, the more this mood change happens. More importantly it's a change in beliefs and perceptions.

Oh Doug. You just fucked up.

Doug reduced his status in a matter of minutes. She's no longer interested in Doug. The gages didn't change on Cindy's dashboard - he's still kinda tall, relatively attractive, seems to have a good job - all that stuff. Then why would his status change?

Perhaps Groucho Marx can explain.

Groucho Marx and status

The story goes that he was a member of a fairly elite club. One day he decided to resign and when the board reached out to ask him why his reply was thus:

Dear Board,

I don't want to belong to any club that would have me as a member.

Sincerely yours,
Groucho Marx.

Meaning, we all have a certain perception of our own status. So did Groucho Marx. His status of this elite club was such that having someone of his lower status as a member reduced the status of the club.

See how that works? Regardless of how elite the club is, if he believed his status was that low, then the club was lowering their status by accepting him.

Though this is a humorous and extreme example of how things work, it actually happens all the time in real life.

The perception you have of your status affects how you accept the connections of people with varying statuses.

In some cases it changes the connection, in others it severs the connection, and still in others it ruins what could be an awesome, fantastic and potentially blissful experience.

SBAAAGMWWAS

This happened to me, and it was really annoying. I connected with a woman that I thought was just gorgeous. *Good God*, I thought. Didn't know much else about her but that from her pics and profile she seemed to be a good mom, normal non-axe murderer, age appropriate, actually single. All boxes checked, gages engaged. And did I mention how utterly beautiful she was?

We connected and shortly thereafter she sort of disappeared. Upon further probing she told me "You can have any woman you want, why would you want me?[3]" It was clear that she was shutting down, sabotaging any possibility of connecting because she believed it just wouldn't work, even though she had a really strong connection to me.

That's not what Doug did. But that is was Strikingly Beautiful, Age Appropriate Apparently Good Mom Who Was Actually Single did.

So what did Doug do? He reduced his status to the point that Cindy no longer thought it was high enough to be worth pursuing. Not only did he reduce it to average, he drove it down to the point that he wasn't even on the radar any more.

She didn't want to be part of his club, but unlike Groucho she didn't undervalue herself. Doug just drove the value of his club into the ground.

Neither did SBAAAGMWWAS (see above for the meaning of that acronym). Instead she just kicked in a protective mechanism that prevented her from being hurt and disappointed by the guy whose status she inflated.

Inflated? "Aren't you all that and a bag of chips, Mark," you ask rather familiarly like we're pals or something which makes me slightly uncomfortable.

Well, I'd like to think I have my good days, my ups and downs and... well sure.

But she inflated it by her perception. And that's what this status game is all about. It's all about perception -

---

[3] Folds arms and puffs up chest.

perception caused by the other party, our gages and our own desires.

Sometimes we make someone awesome because that's what we want. Sometimes we run and hide because there's no way they'd be with us, and sometimes like Groucho we figure they're just not good enough.

You could argue that SBAAAGMWWAS actually felt that - that because I thought she was cool I wasn't good enough. Except that I didn't do what Doug did. Trust me; there wasn't enough time and interaction for me to screw it up that much.

And, that's something that we all have (or may have) done at least once in our lives - we undervalue ourselves to the point that we sabotage a connection.

You see this most often in the cerebral/nerdy community. They make a connection and then just destroy it with undermining due to self esteem, excitement and over exposure to transporter and police box technologies.

This doesn't just happen with personal relationships, but with business relationships too.

Think about selling a product - if you try to give it away for free, or push too hard about it, or allow people to pay you less, their perception of how good it is diminishes. Just like your time - if you are going to do a job for someone and you can start tomorrow on the project they wonder why you have such an empty schedule. If you say you can start in a few weeks or a month, and then when they balk at you it tell them you can rearrange something if they really are in need, they not only increase your status but believe they made the right decision.

If you are available next week for a job, you can tell the

client it will be next month and then roll it back as a favor, or you just say next week and have them less likely to value you you. It's the same damn date! But in one case you have a new client, in the other they go elsewhere and find someone who does a crappier job.

Status status status. Annoying isn't it?

The same applies to relationships.

We see it in the 'three day rule' (which is not a smart rule), and in playing had to get, and in forcing one gender to be the pursuers while stripping them of any options at the same time. Don't get me started on that last point.

If you can help the perception that you have high status you make better and more connections.

No, I'm not asking you to lie. I'm not asking you to misrepresent yourself. I'm asking you to be aware of the system. And I'm asking you to not be Doug and screw it up. If you make a connection, have some self esteem and value yourself just as much as they do - I address this in the "Dear Men" chapter of *The Status Game*.

Don't drink your own Kool Aid[4] or believe too much of your own hype.

Maintaining self esteem equals confidence. Overdoing it is arrogance. And people figure out that you have the latter pretty fast when they mistake it for the former.

You see how fluid status is now? You see how it can change in the middle of a conversation and change your new relationship into a one time uncomfortable conversation?

---

4 Kool-Aid is a brand of flavored drink mix owned by Kraft Foods.

You see how it's about how you present yourself, and maintain a good third-party view of the connection?

Do you see how annoying and frustrating this can be for people who are dating who just want to make a nice connection?

Do you see how this applies to applying for a job, and even making sales of a product?

Do you see how this is at the crux of our very existence and how absolutely amazingly perceptive and important my work is to the sanity of the entire human race?

You... you do? Wait, that last one? Really? Well, I mean I was just sort of kidding, and I'm not that... well, important and...

Shit.

I just did it. I just undervalued myself.

See?

Perception.

Mark Bradford

The Status Game II

I'M MARRIED. HAHA

You're married - happily I presume by the smugness of that title - yes? You picked up this book on a lark, or for a laugh, or you got it from a suffering single friend of yours that you secretly find very entertaining. You ask them about their dating horror stories, and get a good laugh. Sure, you're supportive, but you then go home and say "Whew." Well, that's awesome. Don't forget the anniversary gifts. Remember, it's paper, cotton, leather, silk, wood, gold, platinum, diamonds, uranium, moon rocks. So because you are married (or even engaged, or in a Significant Other arrangement) you don't have to worry about these gages right? No getting in and out of cars for you, right? You figure they may ebb and flow a little but that's life, and you're locked in baby.

Well, if you read closely you know that things *do* change - so much so that there may be a problem.

I want you to avoid that.

So, as I said before there are three complications to The Status Game - your gages are different than his (Tarzan

43

like smart, Jane like tall), the readings on the gages change over time (real life gets in the way of being super fit, hairy boy is not so hairy anymore), and the importance of certain gages may increase or reduce or appear and disappear (you no longer think it's really important that he play a musical instrument, or be such an animal lover).

The Game goes on

All those things are in play as long as you are in a relationship - any relationship. Yes, *any* relationship: personal, intimate, business, family, parents and children. Everything has its own dashboard in your life.

So, don't think that we stop looking at the dashboard once we say "I do" or "I will" or "yes we are an intertwined couple practicing monogamous behavior but we do not belong to each other but instead to mother earth and all her wonders."

Whatever.

I understand that one of the benefits of deciding to create a presumably life long, trusting bond with someone is that you don't have to constantly look over your shoulder. You can relax and be relieved that you love each other - for very good reasons that aren't going away any time soon.

Essentially we trade some of the excitement of the chase for the stable familiarity - new and exciting for dependability. Some people handle that better than others.

I hope that if you are reading this and happily married that you continue to do so for the rest of your lives. If you are reading this and not so happily married perhaps what you learn about gages will help. I hope it raises the awareness of both the gages and the game, for both of you.

If you are in a committed focused relationship you should remember a few things about your dashboard, and your mate with another set of gages.

Awareness

You had a certain awareness of your likes and what was important to you. That's what drew you to this person. As I said in *The Status Game*, there are three kinds of connections we make. Regardless of the connection, you had an understanding of why this person was right for you. And they, you. If you are a little foggy on this, perhaps now is a good time to give yourself some clarity.

If you read *The Status Game* you may have already written down your status items. If not, why not do that now.

I realize that in asking you to do that it may illicit a certain amount of apprehension or fear. Did it? Did you cringe a little when you read that? Do you feel that this question is a bit invasive? A tiny bit is normal. Remember the train wreck couples we talked about previously? These people are particularly sensitive to this sort of self discovery. Their fear really kicks in if you sit them down and have them decide why they really like the person they are with. That is because they spend a lot of time in denial. They enjoy the euphoric kick that giving into a gage gives them, but don't want to deal with denying what the other gages want. Then they get mad, and resentful to the person they are with. Then there's lots of weird public fighting and makeup sex. Maybe.

So, since you are not one of those people, and my question may have only generated the tiniest of fight or flight responses, let's press on.

What's on your dashboard?

So, what are your items? How aware do you feel about

them? Do you just want to say "You know, he's just a great guy / She's just an awesome girl," and then put the book down?

"This isn't for me" you tell your friend later, as you hide under a pile of coats, uneasily eyeing up the book while your eyes dart from said book to your boyfriend.

It's OK to have a little fear - if you have it. Fear means we are getting close to something important. Too much fear means there's a problem. Just like complete disinterest and total confidence may also mean something's up. It's Ok to challenge it. You may really like what you find. In fact, you may find another gage is now present and that he's a nine on it. Falling in love with him again, or even deeper is worth rediscovering your gages, isn't it?

So, what's on your dashboard?

How well do you know them?

Do you have a friend who confides in you? She tells you all sorts of stuff that she likes, all sorts of stuff that she wants.   You're told all these likes and wants matter of factly, as if this is pretty obvious stuff. To you it may not be but you nod anyway because, hey, Merlot. She then goes on to complain that her boyfriend or husband doesn't do any of that.   He doesn't even get it.   Complain and complain - she's very consistent. You just shake your head at his lack of perception - how could he not do this, right?

What she's telling you is that she may think she knows her gages, but her husband doesn't.   And, she doesn't put much effort into explaining it to him either. She thinks he should know it so she shouldn't have to explain it but if she never explains it he may never know it and she will just keep complaining about that. It's wonderful purgatory-like circular logic.

So although she makes a weekly attempt to demonstrate how little he knows about her, you may start to wonder just how much she actually knows about *him*.

Look away

Your friend has probably gotten to the point at which she's started to pull back on some of the effort she spends on her mate. She figures that not only does he not know what she really wants, but she's tired of the effort she's made so far. It hasn't paid off and has only added to her frustration.

What she is doing is looking away from her dashboard. She will - if she hasn't already - look away completely from her gages. No longer will the gages drive her desires, her interest, her love. Instead she will just rely on that same attraction that gave her the initial spark. And that gives way to convenience. You can add loneliness, boredom and fear of being alone to that.

In the best of these scenarios, her behavior translates into his gages going down on his dash. He will also eventually look away from his, replacing his motivation with the same base feeling. Meaning, the best case scenario of this candle going out is that his needles on her gages go from seven to six to five, etc. His status, his rating on the gages will just go down. He isn't necessarily changing but her belief in him is.

And as we learned in a previous chapter this is all very fluid and a good portion is based on perception.

Status and saving your marriage

In all too many cases of marital issues, only one party is very interested in saving the marriage. One person still sees the value, is still in love. But their efforts have the opposite effect - it makes matters worse.

In the case of a wife or husband that puts extra effort into showing the other that they are valued - that they are really important and have a high status - that translates into the other *reducing* the status of the person trying.

Bill and Carol go through a rough time. Bill, having a healthy amount of self awareness and more than enough love for Carol is trying to save the marriage. Carol, however, figures he is trying so hard because she is the best he's ever going to get and this is why she doesn't want to be with him - his status is low and she can do better. It looks to her like he's just desperate. What was she even thinking when she married him and it's good that Carlos meets her in the closet at work to 'console' her.

It's just too bad that after the divorce when Carol runs into Bill he is looking awesome, and really happy and in a better place. Why didn't he do all that when he was with her?

What an asshole, she thinks.

I'm not saying you have to play a game of status with someone you love dearly and deeply, I'm simply making you aware of the system in place that doesn't go away just because you say "I do." I'm telling you that we have this layer of perception as humans that is something we have to be aware of and deal with. It's important that you are mindful of the rules in place. Failure to do so means pain, suffering and a Carol-like existence.

In retrospect *The Status Game and Marriage* may have been a better chapter title than *Ha Ha I'm Married*. Hmm.

Mark Bradford

The Status Game II

LATHER, RINSE, REPEAT

So... Bill. Remember? Last chapter? What happened with him and Carol is worth discussing because it's an example of something very important that we all go through. Well, we should go through it when we go through it.

Huh?

Let's back up, even though it was literally less than 200 words ago. So Bill and Carol had a pretty decent relationship - they rated highly enough on each other's gages that they had a pretty solid connection. But one day due to a combination of things happening in Carol's job, her self esteem and previous experience she started to lose interest in Bill. As I said he wasn't changing, she was.

Lather

Since Bill was a pretty self aware guy he noticed that

something was up. His reaction was to have talks with Carol, and put more effort into the marriage, and into being in love with her. The odd thing for him was that the more effort he put into it the more ground he lost with her. It was having the opposite effect. In the beginning this baffled and frustrated him; he sought out a counselor and did everything he could to get Carol to go. She went begrudgingly, at best. He didn't do anything out of character - his personality and integrity remained in tact - but he showed her (and himself) that he truly loved her and valued what they had started to build.

Again, the more his actions and energy were focused on the importance of the marriage and Carol, the more she slipped away.

This was of course due to status. Fucking status. You see, because she had already reduced his status to below what the minimum was for him to be important / on the radar / worth having / better than she was / good enough / attractive / relationship worthy / worth attaining[5], his efforts just reduced that further. Why? Because our actions always affect our status. Remember the example of the handsome tall man presenting the girl with flowers vs. the nerdy guy? No, well it was in the last book. The point is that the other party has already assigned a status to you. Your actions will either increase, decrease or reinforce that perception. So Bill's actions to Carol were not the actions of a man she fell in love with, who valued his marriage and her above all else. She didn't see that he saw she was worth fighting for.

She just saw a guy that wasn't good enough panicking and scrambling to keep a woman that was way too good for him. The more he scrambled, the more that just proved that he *had* to scramble. Because if he was so damn good

---

[5] That's a long list representing a word that doesn't exist.

he wouldn't have to[6].

So she closes down, backs off and looks elsewhere.

Rinse

At some point Bill realizes that there is a certain element to her actions that changes her status for him, and he stops. He doesn't stop because he's a quitter, he stops because he is not. He doesn't give up on himself, and he keeps his integrity. Bill stops trying with Carol, but he doesn't stop trying with Bill.

You see, once you know you've done everything you can to maintain or save a relationship you are free to now be by yourself and let go. Though you are human and there are always some sort of doubts, passing thoughts and realization that you're neither omniscient nor omnipotent, you'll be comforted by that effort. You tried. You tried hard and that's it. Move on. Easier done with a casual girlfriend, not so easy with a wife of ten plus years and a bunch of kids. But you do. Or you should.

This is the extremely important healing and recalibration of dashboards. You knew who you were together, but now is your time to figure out who you *are*. You can do this now because you focus on you. And as you do that you see new gages appear, old gages disappear and some that change size. You may very well find that at least one gage remains the same. If you think back on relationships you've been through you'll find that this is the most likely reason for a gage being really large and important - because you wanted that in your last relationship and didn't have it. Or you didn't realize how important that was until you met that next person.

If you put the proper amount of effort into this phase you

---

[6] Does this sound like an absolutely un-winnable scenario? It is.

will not only be ready for the next phase but you will become an incrementally happier and better person. And in doing that you will dread this phase less and find incrementally better partners since you offer a better partner for them.

Repeat

So, because you took the time to find out who you are now you are ready to meet the next person. Instead of introducing them to Bill The Broken Guy With Angry Random Thoughts you're New Bill. And New Bill is pretty fuckin' awesome because he was important enough for Bill to focus on. Think about that. Think about how it feels to focus on you. Guilty? Good? A little of both? Maybe you feel indulgent? You'll find a lot of people who seem humble, and kind and successful also make effort to treat themselves, repeatedly and consistently. That's because they are worth it. Aren't you? Of course you are.

You're able to introduce the new person to you - a person that you like even more than you did when you were in the last relationship. This new person also has a fairly clear understanding of his gages, which is an advantage in not only finding the right person, but in connecting with them and making yourself happy.

That's the difference between someone who learns from their experience and someone who drags baggage. No one comes into a relationship like a clean slate - we all have stuff that's happened to us that has not only changed us but changed our perceptions. If you've been with an alcoholic, or someone with anger issues, or been cheated on you will bring that stuff forward. That's OK, that's normal and that's human. Being up front with this information and experience makes you honest and vulnerable. By exchanging this information it helps you recalibrate your expectations to reality and your new partner. It solidifies that the bad experience was connected to a *person* and not a *reality*.

The problem is created when you don't talk about it and are not up front. If you enter into a relationship and quietly believe that this new person is just as much of a cheater / angry / violent / stupid / emotionless person then that my friend is baggage.

So when people tell you it's the size of the bag, or that they have no baggage I have to call bullshit on that. I don't want to meet or be with anyone who doesn't have experience. They may may be a little scarred but wiser. I like people with flaws. How the hell else do you get through life without making mistakes? If you weren't willing to put it all on the line - your heart out there - you're not going to find love. And subsequently you're not going to have it broken.

When someone says "no drama," they mean "I'm not ever going to become vulnerable to risk drama or pain."

New Bill, and New You are going to meet this new person and introduce them to someone who doesn't have baggage but instead experience, knowledge, wisdom and a willingness to admit their vulnerability.

You'll learn more about the "V" word up ahead.

So, in summary lather rinse repeat means: experience the pain, focus on yourself, and find the new (and possibly last) person. It's a cycle of improvement that gives you both a better person.

OVERALL STATUS VS. STATUS ON GAGES

Though I have covered this and touched on this in more than one area on more than one chapter, I've decided it is such an important point that I'm going to resurrect that horse and the beat it to death again.

Oh, my, that's such a violent metaphor. Oh Lord Elcho.

Ok, instead let's say that I want to rephrase and articulate this as clearly as possible so it stands on its own within your mind and provides the proper foundation and framework.

Take that, John Bright[7].

---

[7] See the Glossary of Terms.

So let me once again talk about two things that are named the same, are completely different and coexist at the same time:

Status and status.

Status - as in a person's stature in your mind.

Everyone in your mind has a certain place. Everyone has a certain level of stature based on a number of factors. It is this certain, singular stature that dictates to some degree how we interact and *regard* them.

Everyone from your mailman, to your husband, to your best friend to your child's teacher, to the girl that works at the coffee shop, to politicians in your chosen side of the aisle, to your pastor, to your favorite musician, to your favorite writer, to your favorite random internet personality of the moment - they all have a certain stature in your mind. This stature has an intensity and a certain flavor.

Let's take for example a certain famous personality that you follow and are interested in. They are someone that fascinates you, someone that you'd be interested in meeting. You may look up to them and be part of their fan club; or you may just follow them because they are a very public train wreck and you can't help but wonder what's next for them. In both cases the intensity is the same, but the flavor is different. They both have the same stature - equally famous people in your mind. But one is someone you'd look up to for accomplishments and/or skills. The other is just an incredibly famous nobody who made a sex tape, but they have millions of followers so sure, why not?

Now take your kid's teacher. He's great and he's not only been a great teacher in the chosen subject, but particularly helpful because he was very understanding about how home life changed with you and your spouse and the effects it had on your daughter.

Compare that further to the cafe girl: she's sweet and nice, but that's it. You know nothing else about her - she's a non player character in your world. If you came to the cafe one day and she was gone you wouldn't think much of it because you never got to know her. The replacement is a guy who is equally adept at filling your latte order.

In the case of the famous personality number one, he is someone that has pretty high stature in your life. If you met him you'd be really impressed and so would your friends. If he was the guest at your party people would freak out, and your status would also go up[8].

In the case of the famous train wreck, you have a lot of interest in them, but with just a little self control and lack of stars in your eyes, their stature is pretty low. If you find out they are going to be at the local grocery store you wouldn't rush there. Why? Because you really don't care about them - you just like to hear about the really stupid things they do.

Contrast this. You have a lot of respect for your kid's teacher. You assume he's a good husband, you'd recommend him and if you found out that one of the teachers was illegally raising ostriches he'd be the last one you consider. He'd have the benefit of the doubt. If he met an untimely death or had a messy divorce you'd feel for him.

When the cafe girl disappears you don't even think of it. It's not that you are calloused, unfeeling self centered poopy head, it's because she never gained any stature in your world. In this hypothetical case it is purely

---

[8] See Link Juice.

circumstance. We could delve into how we give people more status, or how the lack of vulnerability played a part in this, but instead let's just write her off as a demonstration of lack of overall status.

Status as in how they rate on the gages that are important to you

As we have discussed in a number of chapters, we have gages for us, and for others. Some of these gages relate to how we are attracted to others, some do not. But we all have things we think are cool and we appreciate seeing in others. They are separate items. If you're seriously into scuba diving you will appreciate and even seek out that skill in others. You may go so far as to mention it on your dating profile. Why? Because it carries a lot of weight on your dashboard; you like it, you put a lot of work into being good, getting certified, and enjoy doing it. Anyone else who did the same can't be all bad, right?

If your mailman is heavy duty into glassblowing, you and he are going to have a lot of chats about it when he delivers the large amount of dead trees to you. You'll spend ten minutes talking about it every time you run into him. Fascinating stuff. But if someone asks you about him - how good his delivery skills are, how many kids he has, etc. - you'd have no clue. And when he is replaced you'll miss your glassblowing talks, but that's it. You may not even remember the name of 'Ol Glassblowing Whatshisname.

Let's say you are Common Sportsman and you spend an inordinate amount of time at a local bar yelling at a TV and discussing in depth what you would have done that the trained athletes who are infinitely more active, coordinated and strategic than you didn't do.

A part of these overly frequent and surprisingly expensive visits is Sam. He's there all the time too and has the same passion for telling the TV it is wrong, and explaining how he too has much better ideas.

You have some great talks about this particular sport. However, you would never introduce him to your wife, invite him for a bbq or lose any sleep if he disappeared or it was revealed that yes it turned out that he is the Diaper Bandit.

"I never liked the asshole" you'd say to the authorities as they investigate his whereabouts. And you'd be being sincere - you never did like him. He had no discernible status in your world, he just rated really high on the Football Fan gage, or more importantly, the My Sports Team gage.

Both are examples of someone who has low or no overall status, but rate highly on a particular gage.

The contrast of that is someone who rates really high in status but not on any particular gage. Examples of this are perhaps someone in the military - you greatly appreciate their dedication and value their contribution to society, but have no clue about them personally. The same would go for your brother - you and he don't see eye to eye on anything really, but you both love each other and value each other as family.

See the distinction between the status as stature and importance in your world, and status as read off of one of your gages?

I hope so cuz that horse is really dead this time.

Curse you John Bright!

DELVING DEEPER INTO THE DASHBOARD

Your dashboard has some pretty important gages on it - like a guide to what you like and dislike, important stuff that you migrate to and stuff that repels you. As we learned before some people just end up looking away from this very important dashboard. But do they? If they look away then why do they end up cheating, and doing things that "caught them off guard?" What's guiding their actions when they do this? Are they actually operating without a dashboard? Wouldn't that just make them emotionally neutral and robot like?

Well, the answer to all those questions is that they actually aren't looking away when that stuff happiness. They only look away while in the relationship they're not happy with.

Visible Dashboards and trust

A wise man once said "I don't trust anyone whose

motivations I'm not aware of.[9]"   You might agree. If you don't know why someone is doing *what* they are doing, you will most likely feel uncomfortable.   That may make sense to you on the surface, but if I go on to say that it's the *motivation* and not the *actions* that cause you to be comfortable or not you might resist this concept.   Surely it's what people *do* and not *why* they do them, right?

No, it's actually the *why* of what they are doing.   This is why you see people belong to groups that do things that are clearly out of the realm of the group's purpose or mission statement.

There are some fairly well known groups out there that clearly do exactly the things they are formed to combat, yet they have thousands of members - groups against violence causing violence to further their message of non violence, groups against curtailing free speech that then do everything in their power to not let their opposition have a say.

Surely once that happens everyone would instantly disband right?   But they don't, and why is that you ask?   Because they believe they know the *intentions* of the other members. And the *intentions* translate into *gages*.   So as long as they *believe* the gages of the other group members match their gages they stay in step with them indefinitely.

Indefinitely that is, until one of two things happen:

1. Something happens that shows up on another gage which trumps the gage keeping them in the group
2. They start to reassess the importance of their gages and the groups actual status on said gages

---

[9] OK, that was me. I say a lot of things. I'm not ashamed of self-reference either.

Makes sense? Let's break that down.

1. Something happens that shows up on another gage which trumps the gage keeping them in the group

For example - you have a big Free Speech gage and you joined this group because they help promote free speech. After a rally in which you throw a flaming table through a window to prevent someone from speaking you look back at your gages. The intention is that the speaker is somehow going to affect the free speech of others, directly or indirectly. So this rally and the group rates high on your gage - they are helping with free speech and anything preventing free speech is bad and they oppose that so it's good and you are with them!

2. They start to reassess the importance of their gages and the group's actual status on said gages

However, in looking at your gages you realize that your kindness/do no harm gage is registering that you participate in violence, to make matters worse the free speech gage goes way down because you acted to *prevent* free speech[10].

So the violence gage trumps the free speech gage. And to make matters worse the group itself makes the gage go down and not up.

This double whammy makes it perfectly clear what they must do. The group no longer has allure to them, and in fact repels them. They quickly exit.

They want to be around and be involved with groups that make that gage go up. This one makes it go down.

---

[10] Free Speech is hotly contested sometimes. Feel free to argue about that amongst yourselves; meanwhile I'm already over here having a blueberry muffin.

Their other gage (do no harm) trumps this gage, even if it's just a little.

In a relationship we tend to migrate towards people with the same arrangement of gages. Or, at least people who have enough gages that approximate the same intent as our gages.

Friends vs lovers

"I want to marry my best friend." You've heard this a lot - said out loud, plastered on posters and dating sites. Mostly by women or men who want to impress women.

You do? So then you want to have half as many people to confide in? You want to remove the only option for having a conversation in confidence about one of the two most important people in your life? If you and your best friend has an issue you can no longer go to your wife and have a deep conversation naked in bed. If you experience some difficulty with your wife, you no longer can have a deep meaningful conversation with your best friend in which he puts things in perspective and potentially enlightens you and saves your marriage?

Upon further inspection, no thanks.

I know that there is an allure to having your significant other also feel like a really really good friend. There's nothing wrong with that. It's a wonderful experience. The point I am making above is that besides keeping them as two distinct entities, they also have something else that keeps them apart: different dashboards.

There's the *friend* dashboard and the *lover* dashboard.

That is not to say that both your male friend and your female girlfriend both like wearing jewelry, being physically fit, being ever so kinky in bed, nature and camping. It's just that you seek out your mate because of your mate dashboard, and you seek out your friends because of your friend dashboard.

Yes, I know that in some parts of the world 'mate' literally means 'best friend' so that's confusing. I mean 'mate' as in the opposite gender you 'mate' with and have kids and all that. So, put another shrimp on the barbie and just keep up with my American way of speaking.

You already know that you seek out the girl/guy for you that rates highly on your gages.

But, separately, you also seek out and feel comfortable around those that *appear* to have the same gages as you. We like being around the same intentions. That's the important distinction here: intentions. If it seems like Bill, at his core, has the same intentions as you then it's easy to be pals.

Think about that, and think about your current friends. Some of them are different, they like different things, etc. What about Crazy Erik that your wife just shakes her head at? Why are you still pals?

It's obvious, you say, because his heart's in the right place[11].

He means well, he has the same intentions.

Intentions = assumed gages.

An interesting distinction between the dashboard we have for our girlfriend/boyfriend and our friends is that in the former it's more of an observation, and in the latter its due to discussion.

---

[11] Let me just say that this phrase is <u>always</u> a red flag to me. When does this not precede some horrible event or large amount of frustration?

You can *see* that she works out, she can *see* that he drives an expensive car.

You have a long discussion over many beers wth your friend over things. You and he/she talk about a lot of stuff. The more beers, the more you talk about intentions. Think about that. As the night goes on you get even more detail into the inner workings of tire pressure vs. surface road area, or fast loading web sites vs. SEO or the specific batting average of Sports Man #34?

No, you talk about how going fast and knowing your car is something that's part of your soul and you either have it or not. You talk about how SEO is all a scam and the olden days were easier and you just want to market your product. And you talk about how someone's political beliefs shouldn't enter into the game and they should just play it.

Intentions.

And you think that Cray Cray Erik really gets it. He's a good guy.

When you are with your girl you see what she *does*. If you are lucky you do have talks till the sun comes up. Yes you do learn about intentions, but you are also with her because of her status and how far she drives the needles on your important gages. You will end up challenging your mate/lover to prove the gages - in fact that's the fun of banter and flirting.

In her case it's where the gages are, in the case of your bestie it's what gages you believe are on his dash.

This is why it's common for someone to have a friend that really is sort of odd and not a good fit for them. It's also why as in the above example some people join a group that is literally the opposite of their belief system.

Intentions.

Sometimes we get it, sometimes we think we get it. The more we want to believe a thing is true, the easier it is to convince us[12].

Confirmation Bias

As I've mentioned briefly before there is something called 'confirmation bias.' According to Wikipedia:

Confirmation bias, also called confirmatory bias or myside bias, is the tendency to search for, interpret, favor, and recall information in a way that confirms one's preexisting beliefs or hypotheses

In other words If we want to believe something, we tend to not only search for ways to reinforce that, but use existing findings and tweak those results so they match our beliefs.

If you believe that Kooky Erik is a good guy because of long beer talks, you tend to ignore some of his stories about women, and restraining orders and so forth. Those women were all crazy, all eleven of them.

You don't compare gages. You don't see that your Respect For Everyone gage is not on his dash. You don't see that Personal Responsibility is not on his dash either because it's replaced with an Avoid Pain At All Costs gage.

Do you see how dangerous that can be? Why would we

---

[12] You can thank this for being the source of some of your dumbest decisions.

do this potentially misleading and even dangerous activity? What are you, some kind of moron? No, of course not. It's the same reason we engage in stereotypes.

One word: efficiency

The efficiency of stereotypes

It's far too much effort to asses every single situation, from scratch, from page one, from square one.

It's far too much work to treat every person as a blank, grey alien with no built in attributes[13].

When the information starts streaming in and it fits a template of something we already know, we just engage the template. People do it all the time in business, in physics, in math, in construction, in advertising, even in building things on the web.

A business will want you to have "3-5 years experience" and a "masters degree" in something, even though it's very realistic to find the perfect employee who has less experience, a diminished degree or both.

If someone wants a certain kind of construction project, it's common to find out what sort of building they want, and fit it into current models.

If the equation points in a certain direction we use pre-existing formulae to compute the results.

A business would never think of not considering the demographics of the potential buyers of their products.

Why? Because of lost opportunity, lost time and lost

---

[13] People who create A.I. will eventually learn this - then we are doomed.

revenue.

We do the same with our brains. Stereotypes, like them or not, exist because our brains found a certain repeating pattern. And, rather than build up a description from scratch over and over again we start with a template.

It is how our brains work - and it is reflected in the systems we build to find customers, to solve problems and find The One.

All the above is something that we naturally use to increase our efficiency and decrease our frustration.

If 1,000 people come along and do a thing, and all 1,000 have an attribute in common   - they act, smell, behave, look the same - you better believe that when the next one comes along you will thoroughly believe that you have them pegged. Your template will be ready.

But if you assign a negative element to every single person that is marginally like a few individuals that do a thing, then that in and of itself is inefficient, because you are ignoring data in place of being lax. The same is true for assigning a positive element to people just because of another element that is present, without really assessing them.

So don't hate the game, hate the ones that are lazy and play it wrong.

The Status Game II

GOLD DIGGERS, SUGAR DADDIES, COUGARS, OH MY

We already know that the gages present on a person's dashboard can vary wildly from one person to another.

We know that one person's distasteful attributes can be another person's main gage.   Something you are thoroughly repelled by can be the very thing that another person is really attracted to.   Some things naturally are polarizing.   Things such as religion, political beliefs and even tattoos are among the the most common.

So you may instantly find that if someone is a devout Christian it is a big turn off, with all sorts of built in assumptions and confirmation bias.   While you may have a good friend that sees that as the epitome of what she's been searching for - a devout, christian man.   Her image of him is just as complete and full of assumptions and confirmation bias as yours.   You have an 'Atheist' gage while she has a 'Christian' gage.

As a side note remember that there are other people who don't use that as a measure, or don't even have a visible gage for it. You can understand that some people are interested in other things, and if the person is sensible that's far more important to them; they'll just wait and see about this whole belief system thing. If they are a devoted husband, caring dad and loving mate, then whatever they believe can't be all that off.

Why am I telling you this? To lay the groundwork for To Each His Own of course. As I said some people have a huge gage for something you wouldn't even have known as a thing. "That's a thing? People like that? Huh." you say, upon learning this over a cosmo.

And, imagine that there are some gages that can confuse others. Wealth and Power gages are like that.

Gold Diggers

You know what that means, it's typically a younger female that wants to be with a man for his money. There are even videos on line (some are a bit dubious) in which a young woman is approached by a man. He is quickly refused because he is average, or he is intentionally dressed shabbily. They then show her that he is actually rich and drives a very very expensive car. Instantly she is interested. She no longer really has the boyfriend she said she had just a few minutes ago. She'd like to go to lunch, ride in the car, get to know him, you know?

Gold digger! Everyone gets a laugh at this absurd deceptive behavior. She was only interested in him for his money.

So what?

So what? Yeah, *so what.* Not all status items are visible and connected to physical appearance - faith isn't, how good of a parent you are isn't, how kind you are, your devotion to saving the planet just to name a few. *Yes, but she just wants him for his money!* You're shouting again. Please, use your book-reading voice.

Yes, she just wants him for his money, just like she just wants him because of his deep religious beliefs, or his commitment to his children, or his commitment to being vegan and his respect for living things.   You could introduce that in a video too right?

No no, you're not getting it, you say.   *All she wants is the money, and if the money wasn't there then...*

You trail off. You start to see the similarity. Remove the thing and the gage goes down. But you still are trying to make a point because you think I'm not getting that she is being deceptive.

Ahhh. Is she? Or do we just try to make an example of this one because it seems so deceptive, so shallow.

"She's just with him because he's vegan" doesn't sound as obnoxious and sensational as "she's just with him for the money."

Oh, so now that I have belabored that point, I want to tell you that I do get it; I do get what you are trying to make me understand, even though I'm actually writing this and you're just passively reading, but what a wild ride, eh? Like a conversation. Neat.

In all seriousness, you're trying to make me understand the very thing I'm going to address in the next paragraph...

Gold Digger vs. Wealth Gage

So you have been trying to make me understand that women who want to be with men who have lots of money are in it for the money, and don't care about the guy at all. As soon as the money goes away, they are gone. And in a lot of cases they will have a guy on the side, be unfaithful and even bilk the guy out of his money behind the scenes. When he has been thoroughly, silently drained of all funds she disappears.

Yes. That is a bad person. That is indeed a gold digger. People with wealth encounter those kind of people all the time. It comes with the monetary territory.

Finally he gets it, you think.

You can stop being smug now - because you have a wealth gage too. Pretty much everyone does. All but the very Ultra Hippy of us have them. Even the people that you think are the least materialistic still have a wealth gage. Why? Because that's how the world runs and they're not stupid. A great guy who can earn a lot of money can be much more attractive than one that can't. Sure, your boyfriend that's passionate about music may never make a lot of money, but he has the soul of a poet. Your wealth gage is tiny and you don't even place it on your dashboard. That may change when you have kids, or have some other life change. You still have to eat, and if you are schlepping it for 12 hours every day to come home to your guitar-playing husband who hasn't showered in a couple days your wealth gage may suddenly appear on your dashboard.

Live and learn, we all grow, circle of life, etc.

OK, but that's different.

Exactly. Exactly the point and distinction. That's *different*.

So there is a distinction between someone who is with someone to obtain wealth and move on, with no real caring for someone than someone who has a good sized wealth gage.

Starting to understand that someone with a good sized wealth gage may not actually be a bad person? Let's go further.

Just like the other gages wealth plays a part in attraction. For some people thats it - that's all it is. If you ask them about it they will invariably engage a protective response - get quiet, even embarrassed. A conversation with them about always liking the 'wealthy guys' may even cause them to re-evaluate their likes, dislikes and beliefs. They may even overcompensate by then dating a guy who doesn't register at all on the wealth gage. And you know what comes next right? They have a horrible break up and she bounces back to even more wealthy.

As I have said before, there's nothing wrong with whatever gages you have, for the most part. Though you may have a gage that's really showing a different gage, or a temporary gage based on something that happened recently, most of your gages are going to be what you want, need and desire. And that's OK. The sooner you embrace and explore that, the more comfortable you'll be in your own skin, and the more efficient you'll become in finding The One. And your trip along the way will have less misfires.

I spent a lot of time defending the wealth gage because you need to be open minded about the gages - yours and your potential mate's. Not to mention your friends as well.

The wealth gage as a prominent or main gage is typically something seen on a woman's dashboard. The equivalent, misunderstood gage on a man's is youth/physical attractiveness. So, while it's fairly common for women to seriously find wealth attractive, it's also common for men to typically find younger, extremely attractive more attractive.

Well, attractive shouldn't be a gage because it's already the first thing we use on the seven seconds it takes to find that face in the crowd for the initial connection.

Ooh, you did read *The Status Game*!

Well, though it is true that a physical attraction is the very first connection we make, there's an added element.

The added element is an energy and youthfulness. It is the various subtle and not so subtle signs of youth. It is voluminous hair, healthy skin and bright eyes.

Just like the wealth game in women, this one also gets a bad rap in men.

The equivalent of the Gold Diggers for the wealth gage is the Creepy Men for the youthful energy gage.

There are a portion of men who will survey a room and zoom in - seriously - on someone who may actually be almost half their age. They pay no attention to a woman that is 15 years younger, but instead go for the one 25 years younger[14].

Once again this is different than someone who simply really likes youthful looks and energy.

So, while the gold diggers of the world mess up your perception of the women with a healthy Wealth gage, the Creepy Men mess it up for the men with a Healthy Youthful Energy gage.

Well, I suppose it's ok for a guy to date a woman who is like 10 or 15 years younger, but he better be youthful and hot himself. Maybe that would seem to make more sense.

---

[14] Assuming they are around 50ish. Otherwise this math doesn't work.

Nope.

If a woman has a healthy Wealth gage, we don't require her to be a millionaire or have considerable wealth. She just has the gage, regardless of her current wealth status.

The same, in fairness, is true for the guy that wants the youthful energy - he's not required to have it himself.

We hope that the woman with the big wealth gage tries to make good wealth related decisions. We hope that the man with the big Healthy Youthful Energy Gage takes care of his own health.

Look, in a perfect world maybe you would never see an older man who you think is clearly unattractive not with a hot young woman, but in that same world you'd see everyone with age appropriate mates walking around with the same physique and financial status. But it doesn't work that way.

And the added interesting thing about me mentioning both of these is that they commonly connect like opposite sides of a magnet. It's common to see a guy with a Youthful Energy gage connect to a woman with a Wealth Gage. They form a symbiotic relationship and they are both happy. Yes, actually happy.

Now you are wondering if the gages change what you see? Perhaps yes. Or perhaps the data from the gages all get added together, and then mixed with varying weights and ratios so that something complex inside us decides on true attractiveness. Yes, that's the way it works to have a dashboard and to be a human being.

INTERDIMENSIONAL MATH
REVISITED

As you may or may not have figured out by now, we really really like how it feels to receive attention from people. And we really like receiving attention from those people whose crank up our gages. We learned about Interdimensional Math in *The Status Game*. Lets revisit that and give you a quick refresh on it.

Interdimensional Math

It's common for people to assign numbers to people. You've done it; everyone has done it. "She's a five" or "Whoa she's a solid eight." Or, "Why is a four with a nine like that?!" Obviously on some level people not only get status but they get assigning a value to it. What most people don't get is the Interdimensional math, which are helpfully revisiting right now.

If you think Sally is a five, and Roy is a seven, then you think Sally got a pretty good deal. If both Samuel and Gwendolyn are a six in your opinion, then they are a good match. So, either one is higher than they other or they are the same right? There's no way that they *both* are higher than each other. The math doesn't support that. One number has to be higher than the other, or be a match. Period. Like if I gave you two closed containers and asked "Which one has more marbles?" and when you pointed to the one on the left I'd say, "Nope, they BOTH have more than the other one does." You'd say I was crazy.

Well that's where you're wrong pal. That's where Interdimensional Math comes in, which is a result of two people's status items being different, as we talked about in the previous chapter. So, if the sum of your gages makes her an eight, and the sum of her gages makes you an eight, to someone intimately aware of both of your dashboards it makes sense. However, to each other and outside observers it will look like one is higher than the other.

Our Gages, Ourselves

Boy, that sounds like a really terrible book. I wouldn't read a book with a title like that, especially if the cover was all flowery, and had like ribbons flowing over it. I'd rather have an enema.

However, it makes for a great subheading in a fascinating chapter in the second book in a series of fascinating books. Also I'm really cool and I hope you think so too and express that to me somehow thus proving what I'm about to say.

We judge ourselves based on the gages we judge others on. And, we judge ourselves on a separate set of gages. All the rules of the dashboard we judge others on also apply to the dashboard we use to judge ourselves. That means gages shrink and grow, appear and disappear. It is ever changing and complex.

But in most cases we add something else. And the

something else isn't a dash of cinnamon[15] or a hint of lemon. No, it's a splash of crazy or a fucking gallon of Completely Unfair Rules That Only Apply To Me.

See, when you are assessing others - especially someone you'd like to be a couple with - you use the dashboard we've talked about up till now in this book. The dashboard. THE dashboard. We never talked about TWO. But you have more than one. See, we build to this. First you learned about gages, then the dashboard, now you learn you have one for yourself. You do.

This is both unfair, and what enables Interdimensional math and therefore love - and why two people think they got the deal of the century. Both of 'em.

When you assess your mate - potential or otherwise - you use the dash we have talked about so far. So when Ted assesses Mary, he assesses her on Attractive To Others, Fitness, and Energy. He loves someone who is really attractive, turns heads, takes care of herself and has a lot of energy. When Mary does the same for Ted, she assesses him on Dependability, Temperament and Flexibility. She loves that she can always count on him, that he is so even tempered and doesn't let the small stuff annoy him, and that she can come up with crazy ideas and he just goes with it. As a high energy person that's huge.

So, you can see that based on this totally different assessment criteria they both rate really high. This means they both feel very lucky to have found this awesome person who rates so high. When they assess themselves in these highly valued gages, they come up a lot shorter. Mary feels that she wishes she was more even tempered but as a high energy person that's hard to do. She feels that she may not be so dependable - based on her track

---

[15] Please don't add cinnamon to your dishes and announce that there is a secret ingredient because all I taste is cinnamon and you sir have ruined the chili.

record - and that her flexibility may not be up to par. After all it doesn't get tested much as she mostly gets to do what she wants and worries that if some weighty changes were imposed on her she would not comply as well.

Ted on the other hand wishes he had that high energy state that he values in Mary so much. He thinks that he's getting the better end of the deal because this hot yoga instructor is with him. Though he works out once in a while it's not at the intensity and frequency that she does. And, as a dude he has only so many options for his physical appearance, while she does cool stuff to her hair, always has pretty nails, accessorizes the shit out of her outfits and is just a master of style.

As an outside observer we see that they are both getting what they want and value. We see that they are undervaluing themselves because they are assessing themselves on what they admire in a mate. They miss the point that they are both equally as valued by their mate for different reasons. So both Ted and Mary weigh themselves and find themselves wanting.

They fail to see how Interdimensional math works because they are not truly aware of each other's dashboards and the impact it provides.

Obviously there are couples that are very aware of each other's dashboards; sometimes that sort of thing comes up in deep conversation. This is especially common when two people are very different and are really jazzed about each other; they start questioning.

When it goes awry is when they stop believing it. Self esteem gets in the way, they undervalue themselves, and instead of understanding their mate's gages they only look at their own.

Being aware of and accepting the gages of your mate can greatly affect the success of your relationship. In fact just understanding the concept of gages and separate dashboards can give you an awareness and understanding that drastically reduces conflict and misunderstandings.

So, when you hear "Someday you'll make a great girlfriend/wife when the right guy comes along," or "Oh just be yourself and someone will love you for being you," don't throw up. They essentially mean the same as what I just explained, in their own obscure, vacuous, nausea-inducing, milk toast, depressing phraseology.

VALIDATION

Now that we've revisited Interdimensional math we need to talk about a key element of status and the status game that we haven't actually named directly. Sure, we've talked around it, made assumptions about it and glossed over it, but we haven't pointed our respective fingers directly at it. And this thing is so important it causes people to cheat, to be madly in love, to stay at horrible jobs, to join gangs and to commit to various religions.

Validation. Ha that was a great reveal eh? You didn't know what I was going to say because I just sort of...

Wait, that's the name of the chapter? Oh.

It's still just as immensely important.

Everyone wants, craves and needs validation. Don't tell me you don't because I'm going to get really long winded if I have to spell this out. And you know I can.

What is it?

Validation means that something that is believed to be a

certain way is confirmed. That's the simplest definition. It means that if you believe a thing is a certain way and someone agrees with you they have just validated that belief. If you have a belief that is not so popular but then encounter a person or group that affirms this, then that's even better. You feel unique in that you came up with / discovered / created something that others don't get.

If you have a number of feelings, beliefs and values that are all affirmed by one or more people then you yourself feel validated. *They make me feel validated. He validates me.* Those are very powerful statements. And experiences.

It's this affirmation that makes you feel good. YOU are validated. Your existence is validated.

When kids lose their way and end up on the streets they sometimes get scooped up by gangs. These kids crave validation and family, and if the gang can give them this validation then they are not only willing to remain in these groups, but are willing to do whatever it takes to stay and not lose this validation.

It's the same for jobs and relationships. Tap into validation and you have a solid hold on a person.

When I first started coaching, I noticed that the vast majority of coaches had businesses that tapped into pain points. I knew that I wasn't a trained psychologist (and neither were most of them), I was someone that developed a system to help people recover and understand time energy and resources[16]. It actually bothered me to see these people tapping into pain and suffering. And how did they do it? By validating how people felt.

Remember the friend mentioned in a previous chapter that

---

[16] Alchemy For Life. Catchy, yes?

has a drink with you and just talks and talks and complains? The more you nod and agree the more you validate her feelings; which is exactly why she's there. It's a never ending cycle of request validation —> receive validation —> absorb and enjoy —> come back for more. Like a drug. A drug like endorphins. That's exactly what it is.

So subsequently I strayed from getting involved in these repeating cycles of pay me —> receive validation —> absorb and enjoy —> come back for more and pay more money.

I strayed from this because no where in that cycle is the concept of *solve and move on*.

Enough about my wildly unsuccessful coaching due primarily to naive altruism.

Back to validation. So we see just how powerful validation is. But what makes one validation more powerful than another? Well there are three parts to that formula:
1. How important the item is that you need validation
2. The importance of the person or thing doing the validation
3. The uniqueness of the validation

Important people are more validating

It's that second item that is applicable here. The importance of the person or thing creating the validation.

Imagine you are a teenager and you look in the mirror and aren't thrilled with what you see. If you mom says you're a pretty girl or handsome boy is that going to carry as much weight as the cute girl / hot guy at school? No, of course not. Night and day. The validation from your parent has very little weight compared to the stranger. What about the validation from a random kid at school that you are not attracted to, don't know, and isn't popular? Probably the same as the parental validation or just slightly more important.

Why? Because it's the value of the person who is doing the validation. But what makes them more important? Well, we do. And more specifically it's our dashboard and gages that do that.

Ahh, you're probably feeling the warm glow of that lightbulb above your head.

So, if your dashboard has a gage for Attractive To Others and that person says that you are great, then that carries a lot of weight. Endorphins are released and you want more - a lot more.

If that same person registers high on more than one important gage - say your two biggest ones - that's even more intoxicating. Now imagine that the gages you use to assess yourself are specifically validated by someone who rates particularly high on your external gages. Imagine how overwhelming it is to be validated in that way. It's not just intoxicating, it's the end all be all. It's End Game, it's The Pinnacle of Happiness. You are happy, you are in love, you are home.

It's why women migrate to Bad Boys and then hate it. It's why some people keep picking the same people and have their relationship end up in flames, it's why kids join street gangs. It's also why people 'grow apart' and cheat on their spouses.

Validation. Validation by specifically empowered individuals, and lack thereof.

Change the value of the person doing the validation and

the validation value changes.

As I have said it is very important to know your gages. In the case of external unexpected validation it can help you to make logical, ethical decisions.

If you are happily married and you meet someone who is a 9.5 on a gage - and he really validates you on your biggest gage - the management of the endorphins hammering your pleasure center becomes really important.

Cindy has an internal gage for Writer, and meets a well known and very respected author. If he tells her in no uncertain terms how fantastic her writing is and is attractive enough, she has both her brain and her loins telling her that she really needs to figure out a way to keep this guy around all the time. Keeping him around means a potential for a constant supply of these endorphins. That can be a problem if she already has a guy filling that spot - namely her husband.

But if she's aware of that gage and how validation works, she can enjoy it but not let it go past anything unethical.

Enjoy the free endorphins and go home to your husband and have wild passionate sex Cindy.

Validation can be a very simple thing, and shockingly - almost annoyingly - can require very little effort. It is why what seems like a huge problem with a couple can be solved by a few sincere words said aloud by a spouse.

Relationships

Remember how I said how important a person or thing is affects the intensity and importance of the validation? I just detailed how the gages can affect that but we didn't explore *importance*. Here's what I mean by importance. We agree that your daughter, son, wife and boss are all important people in your life. You can add favorite singer, priest, personal trainer, and Person I aspire To Be Most Like to that list. These people are all important to you. So thusly their importance intensifies whatever validation they give you.

Looking deeper you may see that your boss has no qualities that you admire - she doesn't register on any of your gages past a two. You'd never associate with her outside of work and if you didn't work there you never would have even met her. But it's not her status on the gages; its her importance based on her position that makes her important. She's your boss and that automatically makes her important - because she can give you a good day or a bad day. She can determine how much you can provide for your family, the length of your vacation and your ability to move up in the world - to some degree and indirectly or directly. It is a built-in importance. She's a perfect demonstration of how importance and validation intensity do not need to be based on the gages. Her importance is raised through sheer status - and not connected to a particular gage.

The same could and can be said for various people in your life - your kids, your extended family and even your spouse. It is perhaps the last one that can be confusing. There are those that lose touch with their spouses because they don't register on the gages, but they are connected because they are married. That's it.

Oh yeah, life goes on... even after the thrill of livin' is gone.

- Jack & Diane, John Cougar Mellencamp who then later drops the 'cougar'

The chapter on "Status Quo" goes into a lot of detail on how this works. Hopefully you got a very good grounding on the concept of how the gages change over time and how status quo makes or breaks a relationship. When this happens you could ignore it all and just slowly and coldly withdraw into your own world - never looking at the gages - only regarding your spouse as your spouse and nothing more. You'd be ripe for external validation that would "come out of no where" only to end up in infidelity and suffering.

Don't do that. There's enough info in both of these books to give you not only an awareness of how this all works, but the tools to reconnect and find that happiness.

You connected with that person for a reason, and may have brought other human beings into the world. Shutting down and then falling prey to your own designs and lack of self discipline which would then destroy what you've built is a fate that neither you, your spouse or your kids deserve.

Now turn the page before I get all misty.

Reverse Validation[17] vs. lack of validation

We now know how powerful validation is. It seems like this drug-like thing can make people do almost anything to get it. But what happens when you get the reverse? I'm not talking about a lack of validation, I'm talking about the *reverse* of validation. To help you understand that, lets talk about what you think I mean.

You think I mean a *lack of validation*. The simple absence of validation is the lack of it. When someone is not validated it's simply missing. If your boyfriend never tells you that you are pretty and that's a personal status item, then it can make you feel like you are missing something. That's lack of validation.

However, reverse validation refers to that overall validation. You know, the big one - the one that makes people climb mountains, cross oceans, throw away marriages, make horrible decisions, make life long commitments, join a cult, or buy extra insurance on a rental car.

The validation of your entire being is an exquisite experience, as we discussed previously.

Remove the validation and the rush of endorphins - the feeling that life is awesome, the extra vivid colors of the sunset - and the perpetual smile subsides. This happens naturally in relationships. It happens when things come to an end, the gages change, a spouse passes away, etc.

But there's a difference between someone not commenting on your artwork and someone screaming in horror and throwing it into a fire while shouting "Oh my god that is the worst thing I've ever seen!!"

---

[17] Another new term.

Reverse Validation

Remember how validation varies in potency based on who is doing the validation? The potency can range from *Who Cares* to *Breathe? If You Want I Can Fly*. To revisit and clarify let's remember what gives these people the potency. Why would one person have no effect while another ruins your life / makes you walk on clouds? What gives them all this power?

You do. And that's the key to reverse validation, and it's why online dating as well as texting is so volatile.

Validation is an active exchange, and the connection to the source is actively managed by you. When you were in grade school they made everyone bring valentines day cards and just pass everyone's out to everyone. A bland, blanket validation occurs with little differentiation other than one card being slightly more clever or one smelling like peanut butter and jelly.

But if you are the girl who's swell on little Robbie, then when you get his card - even though it's the same damn card as everyone got including the other little dudes - you clutch it to your tiny chest like you won the lottery. OMG Robbie says "We'll bee friends forever" and there's a bee on the card!

Holy fucking shit Janet everyone got one of those what are you crazy?

No, she's not. She gave Robbie the power of validation, and cranked it up to ten. The other 29 lame, poorly printed cards Robbie hands out are just crappy pieces of paper with a shelf life of 43 minutes before they end up in the trash in the heap of dead trees dyed red. The one he gives to her however becomes a magic item on par with The One Ring To Rule Them All - because of her, not him.

How does she do this? She plugs her dashboard into him. Her dials do not reflect what reality dictates or what her own perception and judgement dictate. She bypasses all that when she crams the cord into him.

So then what happens when you do this to someone you like, someone that you give all this power to and they *don't* like you?

All your dials bury the needle in a painful choreographed counter clockwise movement. Click. Zero. That's what you are. Your dashboard shows it, clearly. The same dashboard you've looked at all your life. The same dashboard you use to decide if you need to lose a few pounds, if you are ready for a commitment, if you should get out of bed, if you're a good mom, and if life is worth living. Little things like that.

It's a lot of power. It hurts. It hurts a lot. Some might say that nothing hurts more. Some would be right.
This is why break ups can hurt so much - because you plugged in and you didn't disconnect - so the input keeps reading zero. It's not their fault. You gave them this power and you aren't taking it away.

Why would you willingly keep that plugged in when this connection creates this horrible pain - a pain that may have occurred more than once? Why would you risk this?

Because of the chance that you would be validated again. Because of your addition to this spiritual, mental, emotional and sexual drug called validation.

Let's say you're addicted to a controlled substance (which this is, for all intents and purposes) and you come looking for more. Imagine these two scenarios:

You enter a store and they don't sell it. There is none here. That's just the fact. Period. No they can't order any, no they will never have any. You wouldn't waste your time there looking for it. That's the person you like but it's clear they don't like you and you're realistic about it. You move on.

However, you enter another store. They have a line of vials lined up on the counter. There are about 500 of them. The guy says that one of them might be this drug - as pure and as intense as you remember. The other 499 contain a poison that makes you empty your stomach though every orifice at once[18]. You take one and sure enough - you get really really painfully sick. You're in no real danger but nothing hurts like this - even physical pain seems better than this. It subsides, you feel better but you really miss that feeling and dammit ONE of those bottles has it, if you just pick the right one you can have it. Another bottle, and another, now you wish you were dead.

That's what happens when you keep your dashboard plugged in. That's what reverse validation feels like.

You can imagine that this scenario could teach you to rip that cord out of that dashboard right away to avoid this. But some people don't - the addiction is too strong, the possibility is too great.

Others however swing the pendulum too far - they rip the card out at the first sign of this. That becomes...

Lack of commitment

The avoidance of this possible pain can create a distinct lack of commitment in some. They enjoy the gages, the validation, but they are not plugging in or dropping their defenses because they are not going to have this ultimate

---

[18] There's a mushroom that causes this and a guy ate it twice. See glossary.

pain happen to them.

Being extra sensitive to this creates a personality and vibe of someone that is a commitment phobe. People will say they're "not the marrying type" and "he'll never commit."

If you do this but are still interested in dating, you will not only never enter into what I discuss in the next chapter, but you will become one of the most avoided and notorious types of personalities possible.

The Playa

You become a "Playa."

Think about it. A Playa is someone you instantly recognize as someone who doesn't commit. They are out to have fun and have a good time. They usually present themselves in such a way as to appear to be a good catch. If you think of a Playa you don't think of a heavy unkept dude with no style. You don't think of the girl who has crazy-just-got-up hair and dresses in overalls. No, Playas dress well, or well enough. They do everything they can to connect with others. They have style, they are physically fit and presentable, and come across as confident (see *Confidence, Arrogance, Douchebaggery and Status*).

But, since they have removed the ability to make any true connections they just make the easiest one - a physical one. Thus you have a relatively hot guy who just wants one night stands and comes across as a douchebag. You have the slightly plastic woman who comes across as someone you wouldn't take home to mom.

So some summary rules for this chapter:

- Don't plug your dashboard into someone who doesn't want to be with you. This works in a relationship, but once it's over it can be painful. Worst. Pain. Ever.

Translation: their opinion of you no longer matters, don't force them to tell you what they think of you when they don't.

- You are the master of your dashboard. Maintaining a good feedback loop between your behavior and accomplishments and what the gages tell you is a recipe for sanity and improvement. The opposite - plugging it into someone who doesn't care - creates the opposite effect.
- What you think of you, ultimately, is the most important thing. When you feel that you'll know it. It just hits you and you smile, or it hits you and you freak out. Either way thats's a good thing, because it means you looked at your dashboard and your gages.

There are a couple bullet points above that amount to what some would call life changing advice. I'm not kidding. Recognizing that you are giving power to someone that doesn't care about you, and taking that away can be the difference between suffering and empowering yourself[19].

What you think of you being the most important thing really is that important. It's the ultimate thing and that fact is so diluted and so overused it has lost its meaning. The problem normally is that they don't explain why when they coach you, or make pretty inspirational posters, or assign this importance to a gender. It loses its meaning or alienates people because of the lame way it is presented on social media.

I just did explain it, in a way that makes sense. So this time listen: what you think of you is more important than what they think of you. However, we just read about validation, so give that some heavy respect as well. I know how powerful it is, so unlike others I can tell you that what you

---

[19] I don't like the word 'empowering' since it's been so overused.

think is tantamount. But you're not in a bubble, and you can feel the incredible effects of validation.

What you think of you is important and validation is all powerful.

In a perfect world, seek out, enjoy the hell out of external validation and love you.

Don't make me post those words on top of a hot air ballon or a cat or some other bullshit like to make you listen to it.

Mark Bradford

The Status Game II

DASHBOARD AWARENESS

Ok, that's another really good band name.

Remember in the horribly titled *Our Gages Ourselves* subchapter in which we talked about how we look at our gages and apply rules to ourselves? We judge and are pretty harsh and even unfair sometimes.

You're aware of your dashboard, right? If you're on book two then you're probably aware of at least some of your gages. If you've really been paying attention and taking this to heart you may find yourself thinking about this when you put the book down. Perhaps during the day when something bothers you more than it should, or when you seem to get extra joy from something you think is sort of silly you remember the gages.

What's important to you? What is something that you strive to be good at, or be an example of? Is there something you just don't want to be mediocre at or is there something you need to be a shining beacon of excellence for?

That all comes from your gages, their sizes and how closely you watch them.

The shock of awareness

Everyone knows what an 'Oh Shit Moment' is, right? It's when you realize the magnitude of something - something that is either really important or has gone awry.

But let's dig much deeper than that. There are people who have life changing moments. They make a drastic change in their lives - usually for the better. There are of course those that go the opposite way but we seem to never use that term for a negative turn - only a positive one.

We all know someone who had a life changing moment, and in some cases that person is ourselves. I've had at least one - it was a moment when I chose the right thing to do, regardless of how painful, how unpopular, how thankless and how detrimental it would be to my future. It was the right thing and it was the only thing I know how to do. It set me upon a path that lead me to writing this and you reading it. It brought the two of us together.

Life Changing Gages

Most people have at least a modicum of awareness about their gages. They sort of know which ones they have and where the various needles are. Barring the people you know that seem to have their heads up their respective asses and just stumble forward through life I'm talking about the vast majority of humans.

This awareness means that you look down periodically. You look down at your gages.

Example: You don't ever want to feel like you're the dumbest guy in the room. When you don't know something you try to learn it. It makes you feel bad inside if you don't seem to have at least an above-average intelligence. You don't just read tweets or the titles of articles; you actually read the whole article. If you encounter a word you don't know you immediately commit it to your vocabulary. It makes you feel good if someone comments on this, and it makes you feel bad if you ever come off as uninformed.

You sir have a gage for Smart.

No, not everyone has this gage. It's hard to imagine that people don't have a gage when you have it on your dashboard, right?

Now let's imagine that something terrible happens in your marriage. You have always been a committed spouse - when you signed up it truly was for good or bad, sickness and health, good and bad times. You take it very seriously and forever is truly forever. Then one day something changes and something bad is happening to your kids. You try to make everything better as best as you can, you watch your spouse gage go lower, and your marriage is in jeopardy.

Then you notice something else.

Your parent/caretaker/protector gage has dropped due to all the energy of trying to hold your marriage together and your kids are suffering. The needle is going lower and lower.

It hits you - hard. This is unacceptable. So you take action because you have to, because that needle cannot move any lower and in fact you are furious with yourself because it is already so low.

The gage for Parent is larger than the gage for Spouse.

Life changing. You have your moment - a moment that defines you, and reveals one of your largest gages.

That's what a life changing moment is for a lot of people - it's when you look down at a gage and realize the needle has gone down to an unacceptably low number.   That sight will shock you - shock you into focused unparalleled action.

A life changing moment can come from an outside source but in all likelihood it is the result of you noticing that a gage is lower than you want it to be.   In some cases you realize that you have a gage and then immediately notice how low the needle is - as in the case with the example above in which the hypothetical individual noticed his Parent gage and then immediately saw how low it was about to go.

This is another reason why you should become more intimately aware of what is on your dashboard.

Has this happened to you?   Here are some examples of what people say when it happens:

- I just couldn't take it anymore.
- I had enough, I just had enough, you know?
- That was the last straw.
- I looked in the mirror and I didn't like what I saw.
- I thought to myself *that's not me*.

Sound familiar?   Each and every one of these examples occurred when someone looked down at their dashboard and saw that needle dip too far - past their pre assigned lowest point allowable. It made them freak out and make a change.   When this happens to you in all likelihood you focused your available time, energy and resources[20] on moving that needle to where you need it to be. It was a single mindedness that you seldom experience. You probably felt almost possessed and uncharacteristically serious. You didn't care what everyone else thought - because what they thought wasn't important. The only thing that mattered was moving that needle.

You were introduced - rather shockingly - to this particular gage.

I've done it, you've most certainly done it - as someone reading a book like this (self-help / personal development) you are probably more in tune with things like this.

That single-mindedness was power and focus.

Imagine the power of being able to do that whenever you wanted to.

You've heard motivational people tell you to keep your eye on the prize. What does that mean to you? I think Dashboard Boy can tell you want that means to him, eh? Yep, and don't call me that - it hurts my feelings sort of, especially when we are all close like and sharing feels like this.

Keeping your eye on the prize means keeping your eyes on that particular gage and watching that needle move. That's it. Watch that gage, and become intimately aware of where that needle is. You can feel it; you can see it. Maybe it's a three and you need a six. Maybe it's a six and you need a nine. Maybe it's got to be a ten. Or maybe anything above a one would give you some hope? In the case of a recovering alcoholic, someone who just got out of prison, is now drug free or anyone who hit rock bottom, that one

---

[20] A different book that may or may not be out by the time you read this.

or two looks really good. Then a few years from now they are at an eight and helping others who hit zero.

Friends don't let friend's gages dip below a two.

Someone very wise once said that friends are not there to tell you how great you are; they are there to remind you of when you are no longer being you. They help keep us in line and in check. If the person they like, trust and admire starts to act out of character true friends will take the effort to remind them of this. That sometimes creates conflict but is done because they care. They are aware of their friend's gages and they know them so well that when a needle dips too low they're gonna speak up.

Those are good friends, and they help you from going crazy as a parent, they help you through a divorce, they motivate you to stay on track with weight loss and they cheerlead when you accomplish your goals.

And when you start to get stupid they tell you to knock that shit off.

Watching too closely

Everything has duality. That's my poetic and epic way of saying that having focus on the gage and needle is like a double edged sword; there's a down side and a danger.

The feedback of seeing the power and focus when you move that needle can be intoxicating - and there's nothing wrong with that. People work out and improve and working out becomes a new hobby. You pursue some night classes because you wanted a promotion and you end up moving into a whole new career. What starts out as hobby writing turns into a whole series of books. It's exciting and fulfilling.

But there is a danger. That direct feedback can become an obsession - and purely watching the needle is for the most part a very narrow minded way of improving. Just trying to move the needle without keeping your eyes open and your expanded awareness encompassing the greater picture can and probably will cause problems.

If you decide you want to move the fitness needle up by losing weight you will hopefully start eating less junk, exercise more and get proper rest. Maybe you'll take up an active hobby like climbing, cycling, volleyball, etc.

But imagine if you discovered the easiest way to move the weight needle was to just eat less - a lot less. So you start restricting your meals and before you know it you are eating a third of the calories you're supposed to. Sure you're light headed and have very little energy, but the needle keeps moving. You move that needle, eat less, repeat until you are really unhealthy. Your friends at first say you are looking great but then they stop complimenting you. Your true friends take you aside and say it's time to talk about what you've been doing to yourself. If you are fortunate enough to benefit from this new awareness, you realize how seductive it is to focus only on the needle. But life is made up of more than that gage, and the needle moving is the indicator not the goal[21].

Let me state that again: the needle moving is the *indicator* but not the *goal*.

If you want to move the fitness needle then you do the things needed - as part of your healthy lifestyle - to move that needle. You may very well find that you don't need or want to be a nine. A six, you find, is pretty damn healthy and satisfying.

---

[21] This one phrase encompasses true improvement. Worth highlighting.

Understand that a single number on a single gage is wildly ineffective to convey everything it takes to be healthy and 'fit' as part of a fulfilling life. So, focusing only on the number instead of the lifestyle that moves the needle to that number is flawed and dangerous.

Understand also that if you are a two on a gage and have never been a seven you may not know what it actually is like to be a seven. You're only guessing and surmising based on your current status, or the perceived status if someone you believe is a seven.

When you get to five you may find that a seven is not only unrealistic but not something you want.

After all if you have a gage for quality time with spouse and one for fun you only have so much time. Pushing the fitness gage too far pulls those gages down. Balance. But that's a different book.

Gage size vs. Spark Point™

Remember there are two important things about gages - the size of the gage and where you placed the green, yellow and red.

Gage Size

The size of the gage is its overall importance to you. A large gage is important. A small gage is not so important. More accurately a large gage is more of a make or break, and part of your core being. A small gage is an optional and bonus item. When someone says they have a make or break item (and it's not binary) then they are telling you about a really big gage. When someone tells you that it'd be really cool to meet someone who would also be such and such, the "also be" is an indicator that this is a small gage item. You might think it would be cool that your perfect mate also like RC planes. You may be perfectly, blissfully happy with someone but it would be a bonus if they also liked to cook. Small gages.

However if someone smokes, or is a shitty parent, or bad with finances, or not a planner, or overly religious or not religious or really short or really tall or extra heavy or looks like a dude then that makes or breaks your interest.   Large gages.

Just like the car, the most important gage is largest, then the next most important, then the next and the next all the way down to the trip odometer for 'trip B' that nobody ever uses because who cares?

Spark Point™

Yeah, that's a trademark.   Like The Status Game™.   A spark point is the number at which you feel a spark. Remember that any time we talk about specifics there's a part of your brain that pushes back and harrumphs and guffaws[22].   Your brain pushes back and tells you to stop reading, that this Mark guy is full of shit, that you are overthinking.   Note - this is the dumb and lazy part of your brain.   It's the part that prevents you from learning because "I dunno about that" and "It's all Greek to me" and "too much" and "that's just over the top."   Well you don't know that yet but I'm teaching you and it's not, it's fucking English and it's not too much, it's awesome granularity so shut up dumb part of your brain and get out of the way.   You can come back when the sports comes on.

So if you get to know a status item you will also eventually figure out just how high on the gage the needle has to be to get you to say "Ello… what's all this then?"

And if you compare notes with your bros or your

---

girlfriends, or your besties or with your online pals you'll sort to get a feel for where that needle is exactly.

Being out in the wild will also help you to figure out where your Spark Point™ is. If you look at 1,000 women and find only three have that smile you like then you probably need a 9.9 on the Smile gage, you picky picky specific bastard.

If you find that you really like women with "nice legs" and in the summer time most of them seem to have "nice legs" then your Leg gage has a spark point of 2 you nonexistent hypothetical weirdo.

Like a real gage in a car, you have a red, yellow and green area.

The red area is the part that makes you go "Ick!" If you like wealth and stability and you meet someone who has no credit and clearly ruined themselves financially, or someone who says "Duuude money is a construct of The Man" as he gets on his donkey, then you'll say "Ick."

The yellow area is the Neutral Zone of the two colors. It doesn't make you excited, but it doesn't make you go screaming away from this offensive person either. And yes, it will offend you if they are in the red, because your gages are tied to your core beliefs. So just accept that and stop trying to "understand" and "accept" the people who run their lives in a manner that is completely contradictory and opposite to yours. Some people are jerks. Some people are lazy and some people are selfish. That's just life. Run away.

The green is the Spark Point™, trademark and you're welcome for this really cool and neat and memorable concept.

If someone is in the green area they cause you to spark on that gage. If the gage is a big one then this is a big deal. If you have the kind of dashboard that has a huge gage and the rest are fairly little then this is enough for you to really want to go for it.

So if your green area starts at seven then that's your Spark Point™ and I'm tired of putting this trademark symbol on here every time and what have I done?

The Status Game II

PERPETUAL MOTION OF RECIPROCAL VALIDATION

Man, do I come up with some awesome chapter titles or what? You can just see me sitting there: typing away, looking at the screen. Then there's this big smug smirk and something like that comes out.

I actually wanted to make it "The Perpetual Motion Machine of Reciprocal Validation" which is more accurate, but is too long for the table of contents.

We learned about the Interdimensional Math of love and how both parties think the other is the cat's meow[23]. Both parties think that the other is a far far better catch and their overall rating on the gages is much higher than they are. That's what makes them fall in love.

We learned just how powerful validation is - it's an addictive, fulfilling all-encompassing life-enriching breathable sustaining experience. If you get a taste of it you want more. If you get a taste of it from a source that

---

[23] I had a client that said "the cat's ass" instead which is hilariously better.

you hold in very high regard it is a life changing experience.

Why wouldn't you want to sustain that? Is it even sustainable? Those are really good questions that I would have answered had you waited till I was done but didn't, so thank you very much Mr. Interrupting Person. As we touched on, the feeling of being validated is intoxicating enough as to cause people to break their vows, commit crime and generally do unadvisable things contrary to their normal operating procedures. Think about the dad that points his finger at his daughter and says in a stressed voice, "It's that boy isn't it? That's why you're doing this. Oh Kaitlyn come to your senses." He then storms out of the room, and figures it's just his little girl having sex because he didn't read this book and doesn't get that validation is far more than sexual fulfillment and is on a whole different level. He frustratedly just worries and desperately wants her to understand how he feels as the powerless dad, but at the same time cursed her with a perpetually 13 year old name. "Grandma Kaitlyn?" I mean, really.

So then what happens when two people who are participating in the Interdimensional math of love, and figure out a way to sustain that two way validation?

It becomes a perpetual motion machine of reciprocal validation, of course. See, that title actually makes sense.

A perpetual motion machine - people believe mistakenly - is something that runs forever without any input from the outside world. It's common belief that it breaks the laws of physics - like a magic power plant that runs our houses forever. The U.S. patent office won't even accept patents on these kind of machines. The truth is that you *can* create one of these. Spin a wheel in space and unless something comes along and touches it the thing is going to spin for your lifetime and the lifetimes of your great grand kids. The planets themselves are in 'perpetual' motion. The earth has been spinning and revolving for quite some time.

The problem occurs when you try to get energy out of this system. If you make one of these and you want it to generate power it's going to give up that power and slow down, and then stop. The closed system only has so much energy.

In a relationship the same thing happens. If you are wildly in love and giving constant validation to the other party you're eventually going to run out of energy, just like the big spinning thing in space. You'll slow down, and then stop.

However, if the other person does the same to you then you're receive energizing validation too. If both parties get this right then both people become part of a perpetual system of energizing validation. Love, bliss, happiness 'til death do you part. Imagine getting so much of this validation for so long that even when the other person passes away all you have is sustaining happy memories. You're sad they passed but you have all those years of happiness and feel blessed and grateful for everything you've experienced for the last 20, 30, 40 years. You have so much energy and consistent validation that every time you think of them your thoughts don't turn to the passing but rather to the flood of validation you experienced. Warm, fuzzy feelings and beautiful memories.

That's the result of being in a reciprocal validation system that grows, adjusts and is properly tuned.

You have a perpetual motion machine made of two perpetual motion machines powered by each other.

Do people in this situation still have problems? Yes - but

when they do and they see a solution they trample everything in sight to rush back to that equilibrium in a mad dash of high functioning mutual addiction.

Wouldn't you? Wouldn't you not only want this arrangement but do everything you could to maintain and improve it? Ha, now look who's asking the questions.

Oh how the tables have turned.

Mark Bradford

The Status Game II

CONFIDENCE, ARROGANCE, DOUCHEBAGGERY AND STATUS

Waits for little red line to appear but doesn't see it. Wait, that's a real word? Wow, we have come a long way.

We all know what douchebaggery is - which are the activities of a douchebag - which we are also familiar with.

I touched on the connection between confidence and arrogance in *The Status Game*, but let's expand on that and include our good friends The Douchebags[24].

How aware are you of your own gages? How aware are you on how it all adds up for you? Well, in Interdimensional Math we know that it's common for people to rate people on a scale of one to ten, whether they are being serious or not.

---

[24] Tonight at 7pm, join The Douchebags on NBC. Just kidding.

Confidence

So you probably think of yourself as a four, or a six, or a three, etc. And you compare this to people you meet and are romantically interested in. Not all the time of course, just when their number is very different than yours. So if you think you are a three and you meet an eight, you think she's out of your league. Now if you've been drinking[25] and the night is going well you may just try to make a connection and think "what the hell." It will be much easier to muster the confidence if you think you are a three because your gages are just sort of low, but not if you think you have a huge flaw like Multiple Convicted Felon, Horrible Body Odor or Third Eye That Blinks Every Six Seconds.

The magic word there was *confidence*, and confidence is your belief in your overall status. It is belief and not awareness since it's all in your mind. If you believe you are a six then you will exude six all over the place, whether you are a three or a nine. It works both ways.

So confidence is the belief in your status, and specifically the belief that it's high enough. You may call this self esteem as well. Sure, go ahead - I'm not going to stop you, I'm nice like that.

Arrogance

If you believe that your status is pretty high, and you derive a lot of pleasure in shoving that belief in the faces of other people, then confidence becomes *arrogance*. The really fun thing about arrogance is that it looks remarkably like confidence to a lot of people - especially drunk women who are shorter than you.

---

[25] Alcohol suppresses that part of the brain that decides whether something is a good idea, a risk, etc. So you are more apt to do things you would be afraid to do - like approaching an eight.

You've met someone like this - they seem like they know their stuff, or don't display any cracks in their armor. Then after a short period you start to figure out that they are a little too interested in their lack of flaws and the highness of their status.

Or just as likely, you have a girlfriend who tells you her new guy is really awesome. You meet the guy and he has a big smile but he's not really all that friendly - he doesn't have to be because he's so awesome. Plus, he doesn't find you attractive so who cares? He's just there to maintain his high level of hype right in your friend's face so she stays mesmerized.

Why is she memorized? Haven't you read the previous chapters? It's because she considers his status really high, and when he validates her she is locked into a cycle of endorphin addiction. He plays the game of hyping his status, validating her and convincing her that her status is lower than it actually is.

That's the biggest tool of the arrogant guy, also known as the Arrogant Asshole or The Douchebag.

The Douchebag

Why isn't the douchebag just regarded as the Common Jerk? Because he spends so much effort convincing and tricking others into believing he's so damn awesome, instead of just being a jerk. And if he can't get an eight to believe he's a nine, then he attempts to reduce the eight to a three. And sometimes it works. That's why Nancy is with a douchebag, because he spends half his time convincing her that her status is lower so that she experiences more false validation.

If Nancy finds it hard to feel that validation, she's ripe for DB to come along and through status reduction and false validation make her feel overly, perversely special.

Sorcery of the darkest kind, I tell you.

Mark Bradford

The Status Game II

IT'S COMPLICATED

Have you ever heard that? Or, have you ever said that to someone? If *you* have been told that then you've heard that as a response to your question about why someone you know isn't interested in another person (which could have been you in that situation).

If you've said it it's probably because the reverse was true: you were asked why a relationship wasn't going to the next level, why there wasn't the correct reciprocation or in plain language "Why don't you like me back... like that?"

"It's complicated."

No. It's not. Not to me, but then I possess The Magic Goggles of Marcus The Great. Or rather, a certain perception, understanding and the ability to relay this to others in English.

Yeah, that's more accurate. But, the goggles - that'd be cool too.

So, let's discuss this common phrase that you have

probably heard at least once and perhaps said as well.

Thinking about it may cause you to experience some odd feelings - some regret, some frustration maybe?

If this was said in response to you asking them how they feel about you - or someone else - it is because they have two status items in conflict.

If I assume that the following happened:

You are chatting with someone that you like. They know you like them, and you have sort of pushed/called them out on how they feel about you because things aren't quite adding up and you are getting mixed signals.

They tell you "It's complicated."

This is because something about you (or multiple somethings) makes you rate high in their status items (the things that they find attractive) but something else is opposing that.

Possible scenarios are :

If they really connect with you on stuff - attitude, likes, wealth, job, outlook, religion but they just don't find you physically attractive then that's it. Sorry. It's a seven second thing, and just how that works. If that's the case there's nothing you can do and the common response is "its complicated." This is very common with two friends when one falls for the other and the other just wants to remain friends. Friend A (you) falls for friend B (them). You really dig everything about them and one day you either realize that you have some serious feelings for them, or an outsider says "So, how long have you been in love with her?" After you get over the shock of your friend saying such a bizarre, incorrect and intrusive thing you realize they are right. It sinks in, and at some point you reveal this to your friend. Everything is in place - all your gages say she is The One. And you have this really strong layer of friendship to bind it all together. What could go wrong?

"It's complicated."

They really dig a lot about you, but something else registers the opposite - such as they would see you as a boyfriend/girlfriend but you're too heavy, you're a guy and not tall enough, you just don't have the earning potential/ambition. They can't really verbalize this lest they hurt your feelings. Or they are not in touch with their gages to understand it themselves, unless pushed.

You register high on some gages, but not high enough on the others. Or that spark of initial attraction just isn't there. Again, I am sorry if that's the case. You can't change how they feel about that spark of initial attraction no matter what you do and I am a big fat lier because I just made you read a chapter about people doing exactly that especially women and especially related to the Wealth/Power gage so I should be ashamed of myself. But...

It's complicated.

Too soon? Seriously, the wealth/power/ambition/earning potential gage may very well be what is standing between you and eternal loving bliss with the most amazing friend you have ever met. It could also be height, or weight, or fitness. There are potentially a lot of people out there that see someone and find them attractive but because they are one of the 32% of Americans that the CDC says is obese it's a no go. Yeah, not just overweight but "obese." 32% as of this writing. A third. Imagine how many people are passed over because the bonus double cheeseburgers got in the way of eternal happiness with someone whose status gages would make someone go blind with sheer pleasure.

Yeah, no you do not want fries with that.

Before I advise you on what to do, let's look at the second possible scenario for this response.

Ah, Cookoo

The other reason for this response may very well be that they are, admittedly, kind of messed up in their head and really don't know what they want.

Though the most likely scenarios are the first two, let's expand a little on this, because it might have been you at some point and you said this to someone you shouldn't have.

Why are they messed up? Well, we go through lots of ups and downs and transitions in our lives. We juggle our responsibilities and our emotions. Some things require our attention more than others, and if someone is about to lose their job it's going to affect their self esteem and they will put a new relationship pretty far down the list. Or, if they are just coming off a previous relationship having you pounce on the opening is not the best idea. They need that 'me' time and jumping from the protected space of friend and confidant to I Want Everything With You is not going to work.

I know, I know, you may have been sitting by for the longest of times comforting, helping, advising. You earned this, oh Friend Of Friends, Oh Bestie Of Besties Who Also Wants The Jiggiest of Jiggities To Happen.

It won't, and again I'm sorry.

So what do you do? Well, when I started writing *The Status Game* and subsequently the card game of the same name and then this book I made the pledge of not giving relationship advice.

You can put your eyebrows back down, because that's true. I have not given any relationship advice, but instead I have explained the mechanics of relationships. I've explained how they function, the rules in place that we must deal with. I have not and do not advise what you should do to get Mary to like you, or what clever thing you can say to Tom to get him to look past your third eye, or how to pick up girls you charming asshole.

So I'm not going to start now other than to say just re-read those two scenarios and draw what conclusions you can.

And that if it doesn't work out I am sorry.

The Status Game II

VULNERABILITY

Now that we are fairly deep in the second book of the fairly straightforward subject of status I hope you are having an appreciation of the complexities involved. I hope that you see that as humans we have a number of layers, or interactions and programs that are all running. This understanding has to be built upon a simple foundation - you can't just throw all this stuff at someone willing to learn as a lot of it sounds like it contradicts the other stuff. It doesn't, but there are varying degrees of conflicts in play.

As you saw in that previous frustrating chapter, when stuff seems to line up it actually doesn't sometimes. So here's why you may have fallen into that trap, and conversely why you may have found yourself making tremendous progress with your relationship:

Vulnerability.

Oh, you know that? Because you saw the title? Man, I have to stop doing that.

Vulnerability is depth

If all the gages are doing what they need to do, you will make a connection but as far as the depth of your relationship your *vulnerability* is really the deciding factor.

Ever been present when someone is telling you about their relationship? They tell you how gosh darn amazing everything is about not only the relationship but the person. They go on and on and on about it. After what seems like two hours there's something you notice and it sticks out like a sore thumb. Everything is a little too perfect. And it's not the perfection itself that makes you tilt your head, its the lack of issues or conflicts.

Humans are flawed, all of 'em. It's the flaws that make us human, and make us interesting and most importantly to this conversation - it makes a relationship deep and worth having.

Lack of conflict and flaws doesn't mean two people found the perfect match, it means that at least one of them isn't showing any vulnerability. It means that all they are doing is eating frosting, but no cake. They are closing up, slowly and surely because the more of this perfect frosting they eat, the less cake they believes exists. Eventually they are gone die of emotional diabetes.

I can bet you that if you've encountered a couple like this the more they talk about their perfection, the less you believe their feelings are real, the less you feel they possess any relationship wisdom and the more you're convinced you do. We *like* to hear about ups and downs. We believe in a love that also involves some hard decisions, difficult moments and triumphant melding of opinions. However, in the absence of those things we find it hard or impossible to invest in that sort of relationship.

Nothing will happen in a relationship until you show

vulnerability.

How many love songs, movies, books are all about two lovers going through rough times? How many times in your past did you have a breakthrough moment with someone really special and that moment was when one of you showed vulnerability.

Vulnerability is trust

When you show vulnerability to someone they will at that moment understand the level of trust you have for them. After all you are trusting them with this information - information that can be used to judge or even hurt them.

If you are interested in them - or have a friendship or respect for them, or are attracted to them - this vulnerability will bring those connections to a new level. When someone you are interested in shows vulnerability to you it will increase your interest level in them. A respected colleague, peer or mentor that shares the right kind of vulnerability causes you to feel like you are in the 'inner circle' and you appreciate their mentorship that much more.   Someone you are attracted to who shares vulnerability with you more likely than not makes you feel that they must also be attracted to you - for why else would they reveal this inner secret to someone who obviously is into them?

Obviously if someone over shares, or the vulnerability showed is in the realm of something that grossly distracts from the status of the sharer then there are detrimental effects. Yes, over sharing, sharing at the wrong time or with the wrong person can be catastrophic.

You've probably been there - the person at work who is perhaps hurting, or is a Professional Victim decides to be vulnerable with you in the break room. The information is sort of unloaded on you in the middle of attempting to get coffee and now you are carrying around this terrible pain of Cathy. It makes you feel really awkward and you don't know what to say now that you know no man has ever said "I love you" to her. You can't take it and you finally tell your coworker Sharon and she says "Oh yeah, she told me that like a month ago. I think she tells everyone that."

You are both relieved and slightly offended. Being a confidant makes you feel that your status is slightly higher - it's a form of validation.

And now you know that Cathy tells everyone, so your validation evaporates.

Remember #3 from the chapter on validation? The *uniqueness* of the validation is a factor. So even though Cathy is not someone who has status in your life, and you don't need to be validated as a confidant, the uniqueness of the validation increases the intensity. In this case the kind of odd loner at work chose you to tell about her lack of love. Out of all the people at Ultra Mega Conglomerate you were the one kind face. You must be special.

And now you find she tells everyone. This vulnerability sharing was validating - now you feel oddly cheated and deflated because of stupid Cathy.

Mark Bradford

The Status Game II

LINK JUICE AND STATUS

Ever wonder how Google[26] figures out how to rate sites as a search engine? Wonder how people get to rate higher? No? Well read this anyway.

Search results are not just about repeating the same word over and over. In the olden days of the internet that's how it worked - if you wanted to rank highly with your page about pterodactyls you could actually repeat "pterodactyl" over and over again at the bottom of a page in a font that was the same color as the background and viola! You'd be right up there with the other pages that actually discussed it in depth. You fooler. You cheating fooler.

So Google and other search engines have gotten a bit smarter (along with getting a bit more political) to rank things more intelligently, arguably. So they examine the pages to see if you're actually talking about the subject at length and not a big fat faker. Fakers still slip through though.

---

[26] I do not work for or am connected to Google in any way, their secret formulas are safe. Link Juice is a well known thing among Search Engine Nerds.

In addition to this Google looks over other sites to see if any of them link to you. If they do it examines how highly they rank. It also looks at the relevance of the pages that link to yours. So, if the preeminent authority of flying dinosaurs mentions and links to your page, then clearly you know your pterodactyl shit. If Bob Schmugas has a fan page and links to you, it carries much much less weight.

Real Life Link Juice

Status works the same way. Let me explain why this is relevant with an example that will immediately spell it out.

Remember how we discussed the famous people that might motivate you to follow or even have them at your party? Pick a well known famous person. Lets say you somehow get them to appear at your party. This person is also considered famous and your friends would just *plotz*[27] if they knew he was there.

Your friends would not only clamor to be there, but once they were at the party they'd fight to get close to and interact with this star. Once they were able to talk to them they'd actually end up telling the famous person that they were really good friends with you. Right?

"Oh, me 'n Dan go way back, I'm like his best friend ever," they say to Famous Person in gutter English. They also do the same with your other friends and all the people at the party. Over and over again they do this, reaffirming (and in a lot of cases inventing) their connection and status.

Aha.

---

[27] I used to work with someone with that name and I always thought of the other word. Sorry.

The same thing will happen if in this case: You and your sibling have a so-so relationship, you're not that fond of her and she's pretty annoying, you think. In your mind the two of you have never really gotten along. One day you introduce your hot, amazing new boyfriend to her. Your single sister is clearly not only impressed but turned on. Suddenly she's your best friend. She's telling Curt all sorts of endearing stories of how the two of you bonded over and over again, how you went on adventures and how she's always had your back.

Sounds plausible? Sounds familiar? Probably.

She's asserting her status with you, because you are connected to someone she'd like to have high status with.

Imagine you are at a mixer of some sort, and another business owner named Jim introduces you to someone he knows. You and Jim only know each other through casual contact. He's never done work for you nor you he. You say hello and happily greet the new person. It's mostly just another intro to someone who probably has no need of your services and if they did has no budget for them.

It becomes clear that the gentleman is hilariously rich and has a need for the kind of services you provide.

When he explains that he is actually quite impressed with Jim's work, and swears by it unfalteringly you have a change of heart.

Suddenly you are talking about how long you and Jim have known each other, how far back you go, your mutual enjoyment of the group you belong to and your excitement at always meeting the good people Jim knows.

Lies. All lies. All wonderful marketing lies.

In all cases they (and you) are attempting to build a status link with another person so that they have a status link with the high status person.

Just like the pterodactyl web site.

"Any friends of hers are friends of mine."

or

"I'm important to the person that is important to you thus I am important to you."

But not exactly

"The enemy of my enemy is my friend."

I just added that because it's a cool, sort of unrelated concept, but sounds so neat.

So the outcome ideally is that the important person believes your status is higher. They believe it because the people they think are high think you are. And it all locks together in self perpetuating stabilizing math. It has to be true because if it isn't then the other links that are connected to it might not be, and then the whole reality comes crashing down in self evaluation and doubt. So you can imagine that this structural way of thinking and assessing the important things in your life is rooted in sanity and maintained by a desire not to go crazy[28].

Your status becomes higher as a matter of fact. And the higher your status is to someone the better life gets. If you can raise your status with someone you are interested in for a job, a romantic relationship, a friendship, or a client you have a much better chance of making that happen.

---

[28] See chapter called Status Structures.

You can exert more control and have things play out closer to the way your desires would like them to.

Just don't raise your status too high, because it will then mess up your perception of reality, your desires and your connections. Read SBAAAGMWWAS again, if you're unclear on what I mean, and thanks for bringing that painful memory up.

And check out my page on Pterodactyls.

Here are some fun uses of messing with real life link juice:

1. **Want to meet The One and meet better quality people while putting in less effort in your search?** Have your good friend introduce you to her good friend who is also single. You just bypassed all the trust issues, the lame first date, the texting back and forth and the fear of meeting an ax murderer. You both now have confidence and trust in meeting because since you both are linked to her, that link elevates each other's status. You start on date three, as far as status and trust are concerned.

2. **Want to get a job at a great company that is hard to get into?** You would be a great fit if you could just get an interview. Have a friend or colleague who works there recommend you for an interview. The interviewer sees you as having similar status on work ethic and competence as the person who works there. To him you already work there and it's just a formality. Also he's lazy and assumes too much.

3. **Want to roam around in a building you don't belong in?** Strike up a fun conversation with someone in the lobby, and then just walk around. Those who see you talk presume that you know the person you just met, and therefore you somehow belong. Make sure attire is appropriate, unless you

bear a stark resemblance to Richard Branson or Elon Musk. Then you can dress like Every Billionaire - black shirt and dad jeans.

4. **Want better service in Vegas?** Have the concierge make all of your reservations. Not only will they know who to talk to and blow past the gatekeepers, but because the concierge is making the connection it's like your hotel is making the connection, not Joe Random Guy Who Doesn't Really Gamble. Assumed importance is fun and beneficial.

Mark Bradford

The Status Game II

SETTLING

Since we just discussed low self esteem, it seems like a great place to talk about something that is the cause of, and the result of low self esteem: settling[29].

But with everything else I'm going to define this properly, in the context of gages and your dashboard.

If you think of 'settling' you think of a friend who decides to be with someone who they think isn't as good as they deserve, or would like. Right? Have you ever settled? Have you ever thought of settling? There are a lot of motivational posters and graphics out there that tell you it's better to be alone than to settle, or that you should not settle because you are so awesome and deserve so much more. But what if you're not? What if you don't?

Excuse me?

Oh you are listening.

---

[29] Specifically in the context of relationships. Sure you can settle for a cheaper phone, or car, or house.

What if you aren't all that awesome? These posters don't even know you - and that's the problem I usually have with the motivational blanket statements. I don't think everyone is awesome. If you're just going to complain all day long on social media about how you can't find that fantastic person, maybe you need to become more fantastic yourself. Maybe your concept of what you deserve and want and what you are getting are a bit off?

Your reaction to this is to not so kindly tell me to fuck off, right? I'm not only telling you the opposite of what everyone else is telling you, but I'm sort of going against what the rest of this book says, yes? You think this violates some of the things I've said, like that "your status items are what they are" and "don't beat yourself up."

You think you caught me contradicting myself and being full of excrement here?

No. You haven't, and I'm not, but I have to let you think that before we can move on - because it's only natural.

Let me expand on settling because it's really important - so important that I was done writing this book and then it just popped in my he'd and I realized I needed to include it.

What is settling?

Simply put, settling is doing one of two things:

1. Ignoring your gage settings and forcing yourself to accept individuals that don't rate high enough.
2. Forcing your gage settings downward, increasing the size of small gages, and decreasing the size of larger gages to match the people that are interested in you.

Let me expand by example. In the case of #1 you force yourself to believe that wealth is not that important.

Instead of really wanting a seven, you'll 'settle for' a five. As much as you wanted a guy with a really good job with really good earning potential, you 'settle for' a guy with a decent job who is pretty much like most people. At least he's got a job, right?

You are forcing your gage to show a five as your spark point instead of the seven. Or you ignore the seven and choose to see a five.

In the case of #2 you are forcing the size of the gages to change size, instead of altering what your minimums and spark points are. Meaning, you decrease the importance of a gage - by virtually shrinking it on your dashboard.

What causes settling?

Settling is when you decide that your status items are too high, and they are filtering out too many people - so many that you have nothing to choose from. Or you do have some people to choose from but either they have no interest in you, or they are too far (literally) and few (literally) between.

So you change your gages, or at least try to.

Settling can be at the very center of a lot of soul searching, and should be - any time you mess with the gages or the dashboard you should really consider the magnitude of your actions.

Let's define it further, because as I alluded to, it is at the center of a lot of messing with your head.

Wanting someone who rates really highly (like a nine) on one or more gages is fine, but if that is your requirement (ie.e the Sparkpoint™ I mentioned earlier) then you are setting yourself up for a lot of work, a lot of patience, or a huge amount of disappointment.

For example if you only want to be with a millionaire and you are a common schlub who lives a common existence in a common job while living in a common city, rubbing elbows with other schlubs, you are not going to be with a millionaire. Unless of course you register very highly on a gage that your potential millionaire mate values greatly. Then this can happen. However, if you never take any action to put yourself in a position to cross paths with them the likely hood of connecting is still astronomically low.

What if you are not much above a three on anyone's gage? Then this isn't going to happen.

If that is the case and you don't end up with a millionaire, but instead only end up with a man with decent earning potential, have you settled? Or are you adjusting your wants, needs and desires to that of a little something we call reality?

I would say it is the latter.

Feeling bad about yourself after reading that? Daunted? Don't be. Why? Because you most certainly *don't* rate a three on each and every gage - I bet there is at least one that you are pretty dang high on. But I make the point to show you that sometimes the concept of settling - and resulting terror - is used to immerse people into a big warm bath of denial and lack of effort.

You probably have a friend like that - this person complains a lot about not meeting quality people, or more likely they focus on a specific trait that they must have. I had a friend like that - around 50 years old, and went for 25 year olds. He was not a millionaire, he had no discernible impressive attributes (i.e. - no status gages that were above average) but that's all he wanted, even though the only meaningful relationship he had in the last ten years was with someone much closer to his age. He would not be - in my opinion - 'settling' for someone who was closer to his age.

What settling is not

Settling is not being realistic, and I know that the word 'realistic' when applied to your wants for a mate has the same emotional blandness of 'right for you.' They are both terms that make you feel like you're not getting what you really want; what you really deserve. However, being realistic is not settling. Being realistic is just that - living in reality.

Look, I want you to experience Interdimensional math of the highest quality - so don't get me wrong here. The reason the hot younger chick is with the older rich dude, or the solid, boring, dependable calm dude is with the flighty, fun, super fit woman is because both sides offer something high on at least one gage the other party values.

They both bring something great to the table. So if you want something great, then bring something great to the table - something that is uniquely you.

That's really what the posters should be telling you - to improve, to focus on what you are good at and be even better. In the long run this is win win as you become a better person, and like yourself a lot more.

And stop looking at motivational posters.

SELF ESTEEM, JUDGMENTAL BEHAVIOR AND YOUR DASHBOARD

You know exactly where this is going. Even if you've skimmed[30] a good portion of this book you've still been able to see all these building blocks come together. But let's make it even easier on you and put it all here in this chapter.

We learned that you have a dashboard of your gages. You have a dashboard of the gages that turn your crank. And remember, 'turning your crank' doesn't just mean stuff that turns you on and sexually excites you. No, it's much much deeper than that. It's stuff that you appreciate, look up to, revere, and love. It has deep meaning, it is fun, it is a turn on - it's all that in some degree. Some gages have spiritual meanings for you, some are purely sexual and very very private.

Two Dashboards

We learned that the two dashboards (internal and externally used for others) are indeed two *separate*

---

[30] Don't be a skimmer; I typed every word, one letter at a time.

dashboards. Sometimes these dashboards have gages in common; rarely do they match exactly and rarely do they have no gages in common - however anything's possible.

Sometimes we judge ourselves on the gages from the wrong dashboard. In other words we look at the things that we think are important in others, find ourselves lacking, then treat ourselves harshly. This harsh judgement comes even though the things we need in others aren't necessarily things we need in ourselves. We may really desire someone who is very predictable but predictability may be detrimental to who we are. Thus it's great to find a predictable mate but our own excessive predictability would be a negative in our lives. But we still judge, and that's not fair.

The opposite is true sometimes. Remember that the external dashboard is not just for our potential soulmate with whom we will repeatedly mate and further the human race. No, it is the dashboard by which we judge others. Not all the gages apply - unless you are just the kinkiest of the kink.

So if you look on your personal dashboard and then you view others with it, you will invariably find that the vast majority of people don't add up. Why? Because we are particularly in touch with those personal items that are important to us, so we constantly work at them. We know that a five on the financial gage is kind of in the yellow for us, so we are concerned about spending. Or we look in the mirror every time we pass one and for whatever reason we make sure that our fitness gage is never lower than an eight.

Judging *everyone* on the minimum of eight on the fitness gage is not just unfair it's absurd.

Judging both yourself and others on the wrong dashboard

is not helpful, and just incorrect.

Judgmental is a weird concept

When I hear "judgmental" or "don't judge me" I think, *like hell I won't.* Why? Because we are *always* judging. Everything we do, every interaction between us, our loved ones, our children, the functionality of a lamp, the taste of our steak, the length of time we boil and egg, the amount of teal we tolerate in our outfits - all judging.

> Judge
>
> verb
>
> Form an opinion or conclusion about.

See? There's no harshness involved, there's no emotion or intent implied. Without the intent we are just talking about sensory information that we manage.

So that's why I say "Like hell I won't." It almost offends me when they say "don't judge" - like they're telling me to shut down my senses. That's not gonna happen. When you shut down your senses and ignore internal reactions you have to the outside world and things, then that's when the bad stuff happens.

No, that's not what they mean Mark. Really? First name basis? Already? I suppose it's the end of book two. OK, I understand that they mean something else right? They mean that thing that feels bad that the bad people do - they are "all judgey" and stuff.

What they really mean

So, I just told you what people don't mean when they say "judgemental" or "all judgey' or "don't judge me."

They mean *don't use your internal dashboard gages to rate others*. They mean don't judge others on the standards that you have for yourself. They mean don't expect someone else to be able to or even want to have a particular gage be a minimum of five just because you do. Or don't expect someone to even have that gage on their dashboard. Yeah, that's what they mean. I get it. It's still about the dashboards - there's no escape and now that you see it my way you can never go back.

Low Self Esteem

So what's low self esteem then? Isn't it just someone wanting to be higher on their gages than they are? No. Because then we would ALL have low self esteem, because aren't we all lower on at least one of our gages? Would you like to be taller? Prettier? Have better hair? Be able to wear makeup better, wear that dress, be more fit, smarter, make friends easier, have more artistic abilities? Wouldn't you like to ride farther, run faster, have a longer workout? How's your piano playing? Singing? Did you get passed up for a promotion which was due to something at which you weren't 'good enough?' Human existence isn't simply not being high enough on our gages and trying to make those needles go higher. There's more to it, and, that's a good thing.

Dedication, obsession, fixation, striving for excellence and being driven are all examples of watching your gages carefully.

So then what is low self esteem? Well, it's more likely than not it is created when you look at the gages you have for other people and use them on yourself.

Isn't it just when you don't measure up? *Measure up to* **what?** Ahh, thus the rub. If you don't measure up on your own gages you are more likely to do one of two things:

1. Keep an eye on that gage and work on it
2. Put effort into deciding if this gage is actually important

Both are good. Both are healthy.

So, if you feel you should be better at spending time with your kids, you work on that and make some mental book marks to get better.

Or if you feel that you should be great at basketball - but realize it's only because your brother is - you reassess that gage and it shrinks. In other words, you don't *really* want to be better at it - it was just a trick your mind played and you caught that.

However, if you use the gages you have for others to measure yourself then the bad things happen because you can't control the importance of those gages the way you do for your own.

What do I mean? Let's revisit a little.

The gages you have for other people are in place for various reasons; some are there because logically they sprung into being as part of who you are. Some are there because of experiences. Some are there because of some seriously messed up experiences you've had the misfortune of having. Perhaps some of these experiences were rather fun, and hey, who am I to judge.

Your personal dashboard is similar, but there is one major difference:

You can't opt not to seek yourself out.

Meaning, if you think the dashboard you have for your

mate is all messed up you can withdraw and reassess. You can have some mindful soul-searching moments and give dating a break. Or in some situations you may even go so far as to break up with that person because you are reassessing your gages, or found that they've already changed (see *Status Has a Second Meaning*).

But you can't really do that for yourself. Sure, you can pull back a bit, become very mindful, do a lot of soul searching and even go on some sort of vision quest[31], but you're still there.

Sure you can re-invent yourself. You can become a new person, be born again and invent a new identity.

But the whole time you are there, with your dashboard staring you back in the face.

> *No matter where you go, there you are.*
>
> *- Buckaroo Banzai*

So because of this you are locked in to your ratings. And for the most part this direct connection of feedback works fine. But the trouble occurs when things get out of sync and you connect to your external dashboard.

So what happens then? None of your changes are reflected in the external dashboard, because it's not a rating of you, but of *them*. So if you look on your gage for fitness and see a three, and your external gage really values it to be an eight you can work out. Yes your internal fitness needle moves, but the one on the external dashboard does not, because it only moves based on who you point it at. Like you having the speedometer of

---

[31] My Spirit Animal is a Mimic Octopus. Look it up.

another car on your dashboard instead of your actual speedometer. Does that sound dangerous? It is. Does it sounds like that could kill you? Well, unfortunately, so can this.

Normally when you point your external fitness gauge at people you derive pleasure from them driving the needle way up. Thats how it works. They turn your crank, remember? You like hot fit people, a hot fit person walks by and *Hello!*

However, in the situation where your dashboard shows a low rating, and if you keep pointing it at fitness models then you will get the *negative* feedback of them making the gages go way up.

Your device for creating awareness and pleasure now creates awareness and pain.

"Oh my god, everyone is so much better than me! I try and try but everyone else looks so much better. I'll never be as good as them."

That's pretty shitty. No no, that's *very* shitty. That's like turning all your food into bitter glops of goo, with some sand thrown in there. Yuck. You're hungry, you eat this crap and it feels bad.

Screw that.

That's what you do when you mix up the dashboards like that. Every time you would feel the pleasure of seeing someone who legitimately turns you on - the beginnings of a wondrous journey of everlasting pleasure - it makes you feel bad and reminds you that you can't have that.

You're not good enough.

None of us are, but now your rating system doesn't allow you change that, because you can always point it at better and better people, and every single time they are better you feel bad.

Contrast that with looking at your own dashboard - you get better, the needle moves and you get some endorphins and the satisfaction of knowing you accomplished something.

The former creates a never ending, obsessive and painful situation. The latter creates a healthy feedback loop of self improvement.

You can see why low self esteem is so damaging, and so real. You can see why a lot of the traditional remedies don't work and don't even address what the problem is.

If your therapist looks at your own dashboard (through probing questions) and sees that indeed you are good enough, she doesn't understand that you plugged your feedback into the other dashboard. And she's not there on the street when you see the person that buries the needle and simultaneously causes you the pain of failure by comparison while causing you the pain of being not good enough for them.

Does this make sense? Have you done this? Does this explain to you why self esteem is such a weird thing? I am sure you've probably been there at least once - maybe when you are young and immature and learning. Or, if you're not a big fat lier you just did this last week.

So the next time you experience the feelings of being inadequate, ask yourself if you are looking at your dashboard or the one you have for other people. A simple shift of your gaze (from one dashboard to the other) may make all the difference in the world.

Mark Bradford

The Status Game II

STATUS STRUCTURES

We've covered a lot of ground with status, haven't we? We've seen how it affects self esteem, connects people, plays games with your wants needs and desires, and generally is the currency of relationships.

But there's something else. What if you could build stuff with it? What if instead of just being a way for two people to connect, it could be used to build something to rule over an entire organization? Well, you can, and do. And I call them *Status Structures*.

A status structure is an environment that we build and participate in that is built of pure status. You could argue that real life is just that but it's not. In real life you can amass some wealth or resources, and then quietly feed yourself, go live in the woods for a bit and experience some quiet bliss. Granted you exist within the bounds of society and that's all status based, but you are not participating in this psychological construct purely and directly.

However, there are specific constructs that are made of pure status. If you don't know what I mean then you've never attended a college commencement ceremony ("graduation" for those of us who speak English). 95% of the two plus hours you sit through is people with high status congratulating and validating the others with high status - as part of a status structure that is self regulating. The statuses in question are all based on their internal environment they have created and maintained.

Then the other 5% is spent on acknowledging that your kid just spent four years earning a status item that may or may not be valid outside of this made up structure. And they will certainly find out. Unfortunately in some cases that's long after they have left the structure, and long before they have paid back all the money they were conveniently lent to pay this organization for allowing them to participate in the status structure.

Academia is like that. That is not to say that learning and the pursuit of knowledge is a pure status item, no. But the status structure that has sprung up around it seldom is about that. Instead it becomes a self-perpetuating structure, purely for the service of the structure.

The aforementioned individuals who are interlocking arms patting themselves on the back are not congratulating based on what they have learned and more importantly what they have disseminated to the kids in the audience. Have you ever witnessed this? Professor X[32] is recognized because she helped 400 people truly understand what dark mater is. Her teaching style is truly amazing. These kids went on to generate dark matter in a lab - because of her teaching. No, that would be a congratulation based solely on a skill related directly to the organization, instead of being related to the status structure that lives on *top* of the

---

[32] No not the guy in the wheelchair that has mad psychic powers.

organization.

Want another example? How about the church. Feel free
to pick which church. If you spend any time in the
church you will find there is a very definite and rigid
structure of status in place. The structure - like academia -
is in place and takes precedent over what one would
assume the actual purpose of the organization is. People
involved in it are immersed in status, and the longer they
are involved the more it permeates them. In many cases,
like some academia, it's *only* about status.

Interestingly, the military is *not* an example of this. In fact
it is just the opposite. In the military status is not only
important, it is displayed prominently on uniforms. But
this status is called rank, and has stringent, real-world
tangible measurements to attain. And these ranks
contribute directly to the directive of the organization - an
organization based on rank and clear chain of command.
The stronger this adherence to rank and chain of
command, the more useful the members are to the actual
function of the organization. It's the structure, and it is
indeed status, but it is tied directly to what it needs to be a
useful entity.

The statuses of the individuals in the two other
aforementioned organizations are an *overlay* to the actual
function of the organizations.

If I may be so bold - and what the hell do I know - but the
assumed function of academia is the imparting of
knowledge. You go to school to learn. Therefore the
statuses of the individuals involved in the structure would
be directly related to their ability to facilitate this single
task. Do you think the dean of such and such and the
chancellor of so forth is directly related to this task? No?
How about the football team? No? They why mention
their victories in the commencement address - *every*

commencement address?

How about the church? One would think - and I use the term 'one' to mean 'I' in this case, humbly and thereby resolving you of any guilt by association - that its sole purpose is to reveal to you this faith-based intangible fact. You are to be educated and helped to experience this thing you may not be aware of. That's it simply put, right? You didn't know about this thing, so we will explain it to you. Sort of like academia - there's knowledge to be imparted. Unlike academia there is a behavior that is to be learned and instilled.

So, regardless of which church you are familiar with, you will probably agree that this is the case. I didn't suggest anything that is contrary to your belief, because that's the simplest explanation of what a church is all about.

However, there is a status structure that is built on top of that.

Are you someone who is devoutly involved in your church? Then you are very solidly aware of this structure. People have titles, the managing staff of this structure are given more power, and they are revered.

If you are someone who has left your church, then it is most likely because of this status structure; you came to believe but you had to deal with the power structure, the arrogance, the levels, the physical human beings and their ways getting in the way of the belief in that purer singularity.

It is why people leave organized religion and then just tell people they are "spiritual but not religious" - because they still want to believe but they don't want to participate in the status structure. Being spiritual but not religious frees them up to pursue the same thing, but without the constraints.

Maybe your church is different. Maybe it has none of this. I certainly don't want to plant the horrible seed of awareness.

Want more examples? Why don't you look at your own organization. Is there something in place above and beyond what seems to serve the mission statement? Scratch that. Don't look at the mission statement, because that very well may have not only been tainted and rewritten by those who only serve the status structure, but the founders themselves may have been establishing this structure from day one.

Open your eyes

Open your eyes and you will see it.

A pizza place just wants to make really good pizza. A coffee shop wants to make really good coffee and give you a quiet place to enjoy it. School just wants to teach your kids. Your church just wants to make you aware of this wondrous thing. Your government just wants to make sure your streets have no holes in them, you have clean water and won't be invaded by hostile forces.

But then the status structure appears and mucks it all up.

Now the pizza place is edgy, and judges your status based on the fact that you are boring and don't have any piercings. They eye you up and down; the beverages available are only those from people that they know and are part of their equally edgy status structure.

The coffee shop no longer cares about acoustics, but instead about attracting people that make them feel safe, so they make policy changes that makes it hard to have a conversation because it's so loud. But they do make people feel safe, and that safety leaks into their hiring practices.

Your kid's teacher cries at the results of a recent election. She only allows the kids to watch one channel so they can discuss the news. New teachers are hired based on this same status structure and belief system. The new art teacher says it like it is, but doesn't follow the structure and regardless of talent is promptly let go.

Your church's leader no longer goes on retreats anymore because they make the lay people do it. The lay people are more than happy to as they move up the ranks - ranks which are not connected to spirituality or spreading the word, but instead center around power. Now all the kids hear is complaining about other lay people who are leaving

Your government. Oh jeez. That's another book. Let's just say that there's more at play than fixing potholes and constant electricity on the grid.

Do you see it? It's inefficient, counter to the mission statements and purposes of these businesses, and a massive structure built on top of the structures of these businesses.

And what drives these status structures? What locks them firmly into place with a self-perpetuating constant influx of people to drive it? Status and validation.

You knew it was there - you just didn't know what it was called.

Besides an awareness what can you do? In many cases there is nothing to do. If you want that coffee, or that pizza, or don't want to home school your kid, or not live in the jungle then you have to just deal with it.

However awareness brings with it its own set of tools. Now that you've read about status in relationships and organizations you can navigate a bit better. And with new eyes you can avoid some of the pitfalls.

I hope you do.

EPILOGUE

Since this is a work of non fiction this is technically a *Postface*, but since "Post Face" sounds like an epic rip on someone with a long head you don't like, let's just call it an Epilog. And while we are at it let's make it an Epilogue with all the extra letters that give it that old English hoity-toity feel. But please don't spell color with the extra 'u' because I just pronounce it 'coloor' in my mind when I read it and that's just annoying.

We covered a lot of ground here, and I appreciate you getting through that. When I wrote *The Status Game* it was me gathering what I knew and had written on status. I needed to make the reader understand how status played a part in how we connect so the point of the book was to bring an awareness of this concept. Everything is based on status. That seemed like a big radical shift in understanding, or rather, an awareness of an ever present invisible thing. I was pointing my finger at a thing that was invisible to everyone else, and the more I described it the more it materialized.

I sat down and wrote another book, this time about what

life is made of. In fact I wrote most of that book first but The Status Game just sort of came out. Just before that I created a card game of the same name. If you think The Status Game book is flippant you should see the cards.

So once The Status Game was done I took a step back and wondered what was next. Seemed only logical that I then polish and publish the book on Time, Energy and Resources.

But then THIS happened. To say I was surprised is an understatement. Sure, once you build a foundation perhaps you notice a few other things and even think of a couple things you may have wanted to say in the book. That's only natural, I imagine - you can only revisit and add for so long before it becomes paralysis by analysis. But that's not what happened. Instead I started to explore conceptually what I was talking about in the first book. Then I began to dig deeper, and that's when the dashboard materialized. We have these 'gages,' so naturally they would be on a 'dashboard.' And if we have a dashboard for *us* then we have a dashboard for *them*.

Then it became obvious that there were three kinds of status.

Then I got deeper into all those things we consider to be the human experience. With the dashboard and gages metaphors everything just fell into place. I went on to explain validation, vulnerability, confidence, arrogance, self esteem. I could even explain why it hurts so much to be rejected. It all kept making sense - all because of the foundation I built on status and the dashboards.

I have no idea if there's going to be a The Status Game III. I feel like I've written all there is to write on this. But that's exactly how I felt when I finished The Status Game and then very shortly thereafter this all squirted into existence.

We'll talk again though. I promise.

All roads lead here

All roads lead to the status gages and the dashboard. When you understand the gages, the dashboards and how we use them, then you get the fundamental principle and mechanics of how we not only deal with the outside world, but ourselves.

And when you understand that there is a layer of logic and mechanics before all the human emotions get involved, you're less likely to be so hard on yourself.

And like I always say, don't beat yourself up.

Thanks for reading, and making it through **The Status Game II**.

Oh yeah, one more thing…

That chick from the beginning

Oh, and yes, she does find the car that she wants - she finds that people also react to cars that look expensive and not just sporty. In fact, she finds that it turns more heads of people who matter when she's in the car that is a solid piece of engineering. It's a new twist for her. Up till now she just thought a flashy car would turn heads, but after getting into so many cars she realized that this one is just as impressive because of its engineering, instead of how it looks like it's going to take off and fly.

That was a turning point for her, because the kind of people who appreciated this kind of car also seemed to be the kind of people that treated her with more respect in general.

They were less superficial.

Mind you, this car goes really fast and is still really cool, but instead of being flashy, it is *impressive*.

She discovered that one of her gages was actually indicating what the real gage was indicating.

She wasn't interested in a flashy car - she just wanted people to validate that she was good enough to have an impressive car. She was indeed good enough, all along. But in choosing this car she could finally relax and be herself in a circle of validation.

Of course, she made some her own changes to get to that part, but now this is starting to sound like a rather long story and with the added layer of metaphors your brain is going to get mad at me really soon so...

And they lived happily ever after.

Mark Bradford

GLOSSARY / FURTHER READING

This glossary is included for completeness, and items are listed in no particular order.

Groucho Marx - Considered to be one of the greatest and most gifted comedians. He had eye brows that wouldn't quit, and not the kind that millennials spend a couple hours on, each. It would behoove you to watch or read some of his stuff.

Cosmo - Short for Cosmopolitan, is essentially all the things you shouldn't do to a martini. Most commonly enjoyed by women, it has also reached a number of males - both those secure in their masculinity and those that actually have none.

The use of the word "martini" may be misleading in this case because in many cases no gin or vodka is actually used, but rather it is the glass itself that makes it look like a martini.

These are the froo-froo drinks that are drunk mostly for

the sweet sweet taste and are treated like dessert - instead of a way to slowly smolder away as you talk about life, the universe and everything while learning about someone's intentions.

This is not to say that these can be very good drinks, and those such as the Chocolate Martini, the Cherry Cheese Cake and the One I Made Up While I was In Vegas And People Don't Believe Me So Screw Them being most notable. Drink responsibly.

Your dashboard - A virtual place that we imagine where all your visible and most prominent status gages are kept. Like a car's dashboard it is squarely in front of you so that they are easy to see, with the most important gages being the largest. Unlike a car's dash the gages can shrink and grow, appear and disappear at any time.

Interdimensional Math - The math that allows two people to believe that their mate is higher than them in status. I.M. is based on you having different gages than your mate does. You both rate highly on these specific gages, which are different.

Oh my god I don't think there is a word I type that the spell check fails to recognize more. Why? Because I type it differently each and every time.

The One - A common term we use to designate that one person in the whole world that is for us - that special person that will make us insanely happy and fall in love forever. Interesting facts about The One:

Given the number of people on the planet right now, reducing for gender, age appropriateness, availability, commonality, and then filtering further for personality, likes, interests attractiveness, there are still hundreds if not thousands of people that would be The One. Thousands.

Imagine if distance were not an issue because you/they would move, or we had some sort of Instant Gateways all over the Earth. Then imagine that you are introduced to the first person, then the next, then the next, one a day for three months. That's only 90 people. And if they are all absolutely that fantastic and that big of a connection and fit, you would experience something that very few people do - sensory overload and drastically diminished if not extinguished drive.

Imagine being on person number seven and seeing once again that they are just amazing. They are just gorgeous. JUST as gorgeous as the last six women. There's nothing wrong with her, and she's just as interesting, has just as an amazing outlook (if you're into that sort of thing), looks just as good in a dress, or a pair of jeans or a scuba suit. The only real distinction is that she's different and a separate person than the last. By the time you get to person number 60 you very well may find that three of these people are extremely alike - in almost every way.

The person who represents the pinnacle of what gives you a spiritual, intellectual and sexual euphoria is no longer one of a kind. What sort of scarring experience would that be for you? And you still have 30 more to go before you choose.

They all like you just as much too, so that's not a deciding factor.

We could discuss all the phycological failsafes that might kick in, all the psychological summersaults your brain would do to compensate for this experience. Sure, a lot of crazy would definitely be a possibility. Maybe even some self-sabotage.

It would be - to say the least - a draining and overwhelming experience. The thing that we all shoot for

- hypothetically- would suddenly be on tap.

So, perhaps you understand why I'm not a big believer in high school sweethearts and The Girl Next Door. Statistically it just doesn't add up.

But since we don't have personal stargates and there is no Infinite Earth Database Of Matches it still feels really really hard to find them.

And that's what I have to say about The One.

Douchebag - A person - typically a male - who exhibits behavior that is annoying and arrogant. Conversely this person has few redeeming qualities in the opinion of most onlookers. In simple terms it is someone who is wildly out of touch with their status.

They see their gages as being high on a number of levels, and through hype and degradation they convince potential mates that their (the mates) status is lower.

I say "typically" a male because this word is used for males. It doesn't mean there is not douchebag behavior in females. If you think that negative behavior somehow resides mostly in one gender then you're just a douchebag.

John Bright - According to Wikipedia, speaking in Commons 28 March 1859, Bright had not been "satisfied with the results of his winter campaign" and that "a saying was attributed to him [Bright] that he [had] found he was 'flogging a dead horse.'" So, that makes him the originator of the phrase "beating a dead horse." It is worth noting that the person that brought this to light was known as Lord Elcho. If that ain't the coolest name I don't know what is. How can you not merge the personas of Elmo™ and Darth Vader™ when you hear that name? Or a gentleman that always wears a monocle, twirls a cane and has a pet pelican always alighting on his shoulder?

He walks into a room and someone off camera yells "Lord Elcho appears!"

Link Juice[33] - Google's name for the math they use for how links to your site increases the search importance. This same concept is in use in real life, which is perhaps what made the engineers implement this in the first place. I dunno, but in relationships I'm calling Firstsies and No Givesies Backsies.

Pterodactyl - Pterodactylus is an extinct flying reptile genus of pterosaurs, whose members are popularly known as pterodactyls. This flying dinosaur is featured here as an example of link juice in the chapter of the same name. It was selected because I like when the English language slams together a bunch of letters that shouldn't even be in the same room together - like scissors or knife, or pterodactyl. On a sassy day I like to walk around and pronounce the 'p' and the 'c' and the 'k' respectively.

The Rules:

1. **Don't beat yourself up.** I'm sure there are people standing in line to do that for you. If you don't like something - change it. If there's something you do that you want to stop doing - stop doing it.
2. **Your status items are real.** That feeling you feel when you are near or have entered into a conversation / relationship with someone who rates highly on your gages is real. Anyone who tells you otherwise can- in simple and direct terms - go fuck off.
3. **You have your gages for a reason.** The reason may be totally messed up and the result of you swinging the pendulum all the way to the other side, or due to some

---

[33] Link Juice and any Google references are property of their respective companies.

horrible thing your mother did, or the fate of your friend. Or they may be in place because of totally normal and 'acceptable' reasons. Regardless of why they are in place, there they are.

4. **Gages may be indicating what other gages are actually saying.** In other words a gage may really be the result of a true gage. I use the example of a height gage that is actually a security gage. Tall dude makes you feel safe, so it's not about being able to put the star on the tree; it's about feeling like he can fight the others and protect you. Be mindful and don't let that confuse you too much.

That mushroom - So a while back I was meandering through the internet looking for which mushrooms glow in the dark, because why wouldn't I? I ended up on a mushroom aficionado's web page that looks like it was created in the time of Geocities. Among his other accomplishments was his encounter with a certain mushroom. He ate it and it gave him extreme sickness. It made him vomit and have diarrhea at the same time. It was the worst he ever felt, and indeed it was a known poison level that makes you feel incomparably bad but does not kill you.

After recovering from this and an undetermined amount of time passed he did something unimaginable since he thought it tasted so good.

He ate it again.

Mark Bradford

ABOUT THE AUTHOR

Mark Bradford makes stuff.

A few bullet points about Mark:

- The author of The Status Game™ card game - the first and only card game that humorously and accurately simulates dating and relationships.
- The author The Status Game™ - the prequel to this book, which lays the groundwork for this magical environment you live in whether you know it or not.
- The creator of Only A Glance™ - the free dating site that works differently than other sites and simulates how you meet in real life.
- The host of the Alchemy For life™ podcast - a weekly podcast that explores, explains how we use time, energy and resources in our lives. It features guests from all walks of life who experience real ups and downs. You'll find the tone a bit different than this book.
- The creator of the Alchemy For Life™ coaching system - a system that allows people to see where their time, energy and resources are going, make smart adjustments and spend all that on what they really want.
- The author of *God's Jester* - a purely fictional account of a guy just makin' his way through some medieval world.

Last words

There are some very serious concepts in this book. In fact I'm touching on and revealing a layer of psyche and society that essentially rules and controls all of our lives. This is powerful stuff. Awareness is just the first step. This information was made available to me because of a number of things that came together to create the perfect storm. I will not bore you with the details of this and in fact decided to remove any details at (literally) the last minute.

I tell you all of this not to be self serving, but so that you know there were some really hard times - dark times - that created this knowledge. It revealed to me some things that a lot of people are lucky enough to never discover. That's where the best, most useful, most radical knowledge comes from - the places few dare to go. I didn't dare to, I had to.

The inclusion of humor in this book is to lighten the blow, to ease the delivery and to make the information more digestible and human. If I just told you how you are programmed, how there are invisible rules that control how we connect and even motivate us to do sensible and extremely irrational things you would not readily accept that. If I went on further to not provide citations to various studies by Harvard, focus groups, excepts from medical journals, peer reviewed papers or even highlights from Psychology Today you'd have a very difficult time digesting and believing what I tell you.

The humor is required. The citations are not.

If you've read this book thoroughly and paid attention, then it is an absolute certainty that you will start to see the effects of status in everyone you deal with. Instead of just receiving a hint of it when something dramatic happens - a loved one cheats, you're passed up for a job, you are mistreated or treated like a VIP with no explanation - you will now be objectively aware of it.

It's no longer a mystery. No you cannot change this system. However you can not only understand it, but make decisions based on your new awareness.

You have an understanding of the rules, which means you have the ability to play the game better than you have.

Maybe even have a little fun.

Gages vs Gauges

Oh boy. The thing on a dashboard, the dial, the speedometer, the gas thing, is a *gage*. It is also a *gauge*. The preferred and proper spelling of that thing I keep mentioning, as a little machine with a needle on it, is "gauge." So why did I use "gage" including in the subtitle?

According to "the dictionary" - in this case the Merriam Webster - both are correct, though the one with the extra letter is more commonly used.

From the Merriam -Webster dictionary[34] -

gage vs. gauge
The earliest evidence we have for the noun gauge goes back to the 15th century, when English spelling was not yet standardized, and the word in question was spelled gauge and gage with roughly equal frequency. Gauge began to be preferred in the late 19th century for most general

---

[34] https://www.merriam-webster.com/dictionary/gauge

uses. Some claim that gage appears as a variant more frequently in the U.S., though our evidence shows that the vast majority of uses for gage are from specialized and technical industries, such as mechanical engineering, manufacturing, and electronics, and that these uses of gage are global, not limited to the U.S. Nonetheless, total use of the word gage is small when compared to the total use of the word gauge.

The verb gauge, which refers to measuring or estimating, also has a variant gage. This variant appears to show up primarily in informal sources, though not often. Gauge is by far the preferred spelling in general usage for both the noun and the verb; we encourage you use it.

I use the less popular variant "gage" for a few reasons:

1. I tend to sound out words in my head and as I have said I can 'hear' "Epilogue" over "Epilog" or "Colour" over "color."
2. It causes more work for my brain when I encounter these extended spellings.
3. It's one letter less and when you type it hundreds of times it's a savings of effort that I pass on to you, the consumer.
4. Since sources vary on proper use, including dictionaries, individuals and spelling software I revert to the smaller of the two.
5. "Gauge" looks too much like "gouge" and sounds too much like "gauze" in my head, so I don't want to keep thinking about poking or bandages every time I encounter that word.

So, that is why I went with the shorter, less preferred but more efficient and informal "gage."

Find me

To keep track of all things related to The Status Game, including new books and the card game, go to **thestatusgame.com**, follow me on instagram @thestatusgame.

Check out **thestatusgame.com** for worksheets and bonus items related to the books and the card game. Make sure you add yourself to the mailing list for promotions, free items and announcements. Reach out to me for comments on the books and the game. I want to hear from you!

My Alchemy For Life Podcast is on iTunes, Google Play, TuneIn, last.fm, and many others.

Search "Alchemy For Life" in your podcast software, or go to **alchemyfor.life**, follow on instagram @alchemyforlife

Psssst…. I like to cross promote my stuff, so rating the podcast sometimes gets you a signed copy of a book, rating the book on Amazon sometimes gets you a signed copy of the card game, rating the card game sometimes gets you a signed copy of the book, etc.

It's my way of thanking you.

The Status Game II

Mark Bradford